Martin Kramer
EDITOR-IN-CHIEF

Technology Leadership: Communication and Information Systems in Higher Education

George R. Maughan
West Virginia University

EDITOR

Number 115, Fall 2001

JOSSEY-BASS
San Francisco

TECHNOLOGY LEADERSHIP:
COMMUNICATION AND INFORMATION SYSTEMS IN HIGHER EDUCATION
George R. Maughan (ed.)
New Directions for Higher Education, no. 115
Martin Kramer, Editor-in-Chief

Microfilm copies of issues and articles are available in 16mm and 35mm, as well as microfiche in 105mm, through University Microfilms Inc., 300 North Zeeb Road, Ann Arbor, Michigan 48106-1346.

ISSN 0271-0560   electronic ISSN 1534-2883   ISBN 0-7879-5783-6

NEW DIRECTIONS FOR HIGHER EDUCATION is part of The Jossey-Bass Higher and Adult Education Series and is published quarterly by Jossey-Bass. 989 Market Street, San Francisco, California 94103-1741. Periodicals postage paid at San Francisco, California, and at additional mailing offices. Postmaster: Send address changes to New Directions for Higher Education, Jossey-Bass, 989 Market Street, San Francisco, California 94103-1741.

SUBSCRIPTIONS cost $63 for individuals and $138 for institutions, agencies, and libraries. See ordering information page at end of book.

EDITORIAL CORRESPONDENCE should be sent to the Editor-in-Chief, Martin Kramer, 2807 Shasta Road, Berkeley, California 94708-2011.

Cover photograph and random dot by Richard Blair/Color & Light © 1990.

Jossey-Bass Web address: www.josseybass.com

Printed in the United States of America on acid-free recycled paper containing 100 percent recovered waste paper, of which at least 20 percent is postconsumer waste.

Contents

EDITOR'S NOTES

Communication and information systems are transforming technologies, changing the very nature of higher education. Legacy and new networks coexist or converge to provide access and perform information transfer, storage retrieval, and processing essential to the functions of the modern campus. Because of this transformation, insightful technology leadership is required of administrators, faculty, and staff to achieve the goals of the institution.

In this volume, we describe and explain the nature of the communication and information systems infrastructure on higher education campuses, examine the impact of these systems on the basic functions of higher education institutions, show how communication and information systems relate to the day-to-day responsibilities of campus administrators and leaders, and familiarize administrators with concepts and terms they may not fully understand.

Throughout this volume, emphasis is placed on a systems perspective. A communication and information systems infrastructure model is established to focus the reader on the context of information technology (IT) in the modern campus and the devices, networks, skills, budget, and policy elements of the infrastructure. The content treatment is designed for readers who have a limited or intermediate technical background.

This volume first covers the nature of the modern campus (Chapter One) and explains a communication and information systems infrastructure model (Chapter Two). The five major infrastructure elements are then addressed individually (devices, Chapter Three; networks, Chapter Four; skills, Chapter Five; budget, Chapter Six; and policies, Chapter Seven). The topic of technology leadership is addressed in Chapter Eight. Finally, changing practices and new frontiers as a result of communication and information systems are synthesized and explored in Chapter Nine.

George R. Maughan
Editor

GEORGE R. MAUGHAN is associate professor of technology education and coordinator of the communication and information systems sequence of study at West Virginia University, Morgantown, West Virginia.

NEW DIRECTIONS FOR HIGHER EDUCATION, no. 115, Fall 2001 © John Wiley & Sons, Inc.

1

The modern campus is a learning environment of unprecedented flexibility and effectiveness that respects and treasures the academic values and traditions of the past while embracing the technological tools of the present.

The Modern Campus

Donald N. Langenberg, Donald Z. Spicer

Connecting teachers with learners is the essence of the academy. When the dominant mode of transmitting knowledge was oral and the number of teachers and learners was small, as in Plato's Academy, that often meant one teacher speaking directly with a few students, perhaps just one on the other end of the teacher's log. As the number of teachers and learners grew in medieval Europe, they began to band together in colleges and universities, housed in buildings typically scattered throughout a city.

The advent of printing transformed the nature of the academy, making feasible and efficient the connection of teachers (in other words, the authors of books) with learners separated from them in both time and space. It also made a library the essential key physical asset of any college or university.

When the American colonists began to create their own colleges and universities, they often found it convenient to do so on undeveloped land outside preexisting cities. Thus, it was natural to adapt the Latin word *campus* (meaning "field" or "plain") to describe the physical facilities of the college or university. To this day, the popular image of the ideal university is a green, leafy quadrangle surrounded by stately academic buildings, including a large library.

During the previous century, U.S. colleges and universities underwent radical change. A college or university degree became the sine qua non for admission into (and often, continued participation in) the white-collar workforce as well as a necessity for informed participation in society. Scientific, technological, and social innovations emanating from U.S. higher education institutions fueled much of our nation's social and economic progress during the twentieth century. They included an innovation comparable in importance to printing, information technology (IT), based on computers and telecommunications. Now, at the dawn of a new century, IT continues to develop at a steadily quickening pace.

In light of these developments, what might one expect the typical college or university campus to look like in the early decades of the twenty-first century? In this chapter we attempt a brief description of what might plausibly occur within the lifetimes of most readers, with emphasis on those changes most likely to be rendered feasible—and driven—by IT advances.

New Models

In the United States, many different types of higher education institutions evolved in response to the evolving societal needs of the twentieth century. The Carnegie Foundation for the Advancement of Teaching now classifies the approximately thirty-six hundred institutions of higher education in the United States into ten broad types. Thus, the twenty-first-century campus cannot be described in terms of a single model. Nevertheless, there remain some common denominators shared by most if not all of U.S. higher education institutions.

Higher education serves the broadly accepted functions of creation, transmission, preservation, and application of knowledge. Consequently, almost every higher education institution articulates missions of teaching and learning, research, and community service. The activities related to achieving these missions have been given different weights by different institutions. In some, aspirations to move toward a larger research-oriented role, driven in part by outside funding opportunities, have tended to shift the balance of their activities. The question of what should be the appropriate balance is a persistent feature of intra-institutional debate in most colleges and universities.

With the continuing growth of a knowledge-based society, changing demographics in learners, competition from for-profit entities, and the growth of opportunities to commercialize research findings, the diversity of twenty-first-century higher education institutions is likely to become even greater than it was in the twentieth century. In the insightful article *A Choice of Transformations for the Twenty-First-Century University,* Duderstadt (2000) describes nine models for future higher education institutions. In the decades to come, institutions may continue to try to balance the demands of several of these models, but it is increasingly clear that even the largest and most diverse them can no longer be all things to all people. Defining the modern campus thus requires multiple descriptions, perhaps even a different one for each of our approximately thirty-six hundred institutions. Here, however, we will focus on the commonalities among higher education institutions rather than on their differences.

By the end of the twentieth century, essentially all higher education institutions had developed some common IT infrastructure components.

The increasing societal importance of higher education has driven its institutional diversification, which has been enabled by IT. For example, on-line universities are an outgrowth of the pervasiveness of the Internet and the new tools it provides in support of teaching and learning.

In addition to common components, there have been some common trends related to integration of components and convergence of technologies. IT remains an immature and rapidly evolving field in which significant changes occur every decade. (Remember that the Internet, which is now an integral feature of all our lives, is less than a decade old.) The effective lifetime of IT investments is often measured in terms of periods of three to five years, and this is likely to continue for the foreseeable future. Moore's Law, which holds that the number of transistors per integrated circuit will double every eighteen months, seems to have held in the microprocessor business for over thirty-five years and has effected change in every business that depends on computers as well. Although significant changes in higher education institutions normally occur in time scales reminiscent of plate tectonic movement, the wide adoption of microcomputers, the Internet, and the World Wide Web in the last decade has inspired serious rethinking of the models that underlie this field. Table 1.1 presents some examples of projected or observable changes.

Scenario

Perhaps the best way to understand the interaction between IT and the modern campus is to imagine being a member of a university community a little later in the early twenty-first century. This scenario describes what it would be like to be a student or a faculty member at an institution that is doing everything right in terms of technology available today or foreseeable tomorrow. Many of the most interesting IT components mentioned in this section are just coming onto the market, but nothing is beyond the scope of full deployment by 2005.

The Student. Mary is a freshman. She has been on campus for close to two months now. Although she had used her own personal computer at home all through high school and her teachers had increasingly used on-line resources as an integral part of her education, she is finding the university to be light-years ahead of anything she had experienced.

Members of her entering class were the first to be required to purchase wireless digital assistants. This book-sized computing device is set up to look first at her personal university portal (PUP). From anywhere on campus she can communicate with classmates and faculty, take a preliminary look at the notes and materials that the professor in her next class will be discussing, and access library materials. In fact, many of her textbooks have been downloaded into the digital assistant as well so that she has all of her materials wherever she is.

Table 1.1. Changing Models in Higher Education

	Old Model	New Model
Teaching/learning	Learner comes to a classroom on a campus.	Learning resources available wherever the learner is.
	Classes are scheduled.	Learning is available whenever learner wishes.
	Teaching to the middle of the class.	Learning environment is personalized to the learner.
	Learning is individual activity.	Learning is collaborative activity.
	Classes are custom designed and offered by an individual faculty member for a single class of students. Materials may be partially reused by that faculty member in a later class offering.	Classes are constructed from modular learning objects that can be shared broadly by faculty members participating in a microcommerce of such components.
Research	Collaboration is even driven (at conferences, scheduled phone or face-to-face meetings, and so on).	Collaboration is ad hoc, continuous, and technology enabled.
	Researchers go to specialized resources (high-energy accelerators, supercomputer centers, observatories, and so on).	Researchers control instruments and collect data from their offices.
Partnerships	University focused on pure research.	University also engaged in applied research.
	University at arm's length from commercializing products.	University is a parner in incubating innovative businesses.
	University provides itself all needed services.	University manages contracts for services.
Community service	Emanating from campus and extension services; provided by specialized faculty and staff.	Pervasive—anytime and anywhere—provided by everybody.
Libraries	The physical library as heart of the campus.	The digital library accessible anytime and anywhere by anyone who qualifies under the license to use.
Managing the enterprise	Services highly intermediated and place based.	Self-service on an anytime-anywhere model.
	Decisions based on available fragments of information.	Decisions based on comprehensive analytical data.
	Commercial transactions are paper and credit card.	Commercial transactions are electronic.

(*continued*)

Table 1.1. (*continued*)

	Old Model	New Model
Managing the enterprise (*continued*)	Support services provided by institutional staff.	Outsource nonstrategic services that are not core institutional capabilities.
Collaboration	Each institution is autonomous and provides whatever is necessary for its community. Competition rules, and collaboration is viewed as an unnatural act.	*Collabotition* (collaboration + competition)—no institution can do it all any longer. Form cooperative arrangements with traditionally competing institutions.

The first thing she did upon receiving her digital assistant was to personalize her PUP so that she can not only access all her classes but also follow her favorite sports, read her hometown newspaper, and be alerted when her financial aid is electronically deposited into her university account. The university can automatically augment her to-do list with the academic calendar, including registration and payment deadlines. Her personal assistant will notify her of upcoming events based on her stated preferences or her prior expressed interests.

The time to register for spring semester is quickly approaching, and Mary, a prospective education major, has already had numerous communications and a visit with her faculty adviser. She can register through her digital assistant, which will alert her when her scheduled registration time is approaching. Mary's registration activity will be monitored by a smart system that is no longer just a passive receiver of transactions. This system automatically links her degree progress status to her course selections and will warn her if she is not registered for a needed course. If Mary does not register for enough credits to maintain her scholarship eligibility, the smart system can analyze her individual financial aid files and will remind her that her credit load is not adequate. Once registered, Mary can order her hardcopy books directly from the bookstore or download text directly into her personal assistant. The presence of her course syllabi will allow Mary's personal calendar to be updated with class meeting times and places, exam dates, research deadlines, and other assignments. She will be automatically enrolled in required course chat rooms and be placed on her teacher's e-mail distribution lists.

Her classroom discussions are always lively, and because each student has a digital assistant, there is no need to focus on taking notes. Therefore, each student can participate fully in the dialogue. The materials are available in a variety of formats on a campus server. Additionally, the observations her professors write on blackboards can easily be downloaded into each student's digital assistant after class, thanks to the technology built into her university's smart classrooms. More formal lectures, including those given by distinguished visitors, are videotaped and are viewable on demand at any time over the campus high-speed network. Mary has a more traditional computer in her dorm room that is connected to this network and that synchronizes information with her digital assistant.

The university has created an environment where she can focus on learning and living. She spends little time on the "administrivia" of managing her life on campus; instead, she is able to fully immerse herself in a world of ideas. More importantly, she has the tools to access and organize those ideas as well as to communicate with the members of her new community. Mary may not realize it, but she is benefiting from the integration of technology and teaching, an experience that will serve her well in a few years when she stands before her own students (whether literally or virtually).

The Faculty Member. Professor Land has been at the university for many years. Although he was educated in the last half of the twentieth century, he has to concede that the twenty-first century has yielded developments that have made him a better teacher and researcher.

Professor Land started his career developing classroom lectures, as his professors had done before him, and he still occasionally teaches a course in lecture format when appropriate. But over time he has become convinced that a more interactive style—one in which teams of students work collaboratively—is better in many courses. His role has shifted: no longer is he the source of all knowledge but instead the knowledgeable mentor and learning facilitator.

The university has provided many electronic tools to enable these changes to occur. Although classroom discussions still play an important role in understanding complex issues, students spend much more time communicating electronically outside of class. His course materials are always available on-line to members of each of his classes. At first, creating these materials in electronic format was time consuming, but the university offered support and training to simplify the job. Easy-to-use course development and course management tools were licensed for all faculty members. Training in how to use these tools, and more important, in how to create a learning environment in an electronic medium, was provided. And because electronic media are increasingly critical to teaching and learning, the university has made certain that support services function—and function well—all of the time.

It has become clear that the old model—that of each professor creating the materials for a course, teaching it once for a class, and then repeating it for another class—is not an efficient use of resources either by the professor or the university. In the new paradigm, Professor Land's university has collaborated with other institutions to create an exchange of course objects—small learning units that a professor created for a particular course but that may be used by another professor in another course. They are somewhat analogous to the components of the course packs that Professor Land used when he was a student. However, in the electronic world, these course objects can contain simulations, animations, and video clips as well as high-production-quality pictures and text.

Because of the investments in IT networks that the university has made, Professor Land is able to work much more collaboratively with industries that are interested in his research. He holds video chat sessions twice a semester with employees at a new company across the state. The company relies on Professor Land's expertise and that of several of his colleagues to help solve productivity problems. In turn, Professor Land can reflect the company's real-world experiences in his teaching on campus, further preparing his students for what they will find in the workplace. Occasionally, he connects the two groups—through technology.

Professor Land's research activities have also been significantly affected by the availability of electronic services. His graduate students now submit theses and dissertations electronically rather than on paper. This allows them to be much richer documents, showing videos of an experiment, for example, in addition to the outcomes of the experiment. Statistical analyses can be run within the dissertation as the parameters of an experiment are changed. These theses, together with a wide range of electronic materials, are available to all in the discipline once they are submitted to the Regional Digital Library.

When Professor Land cannot attend conferences, he can participate in sessions via videoconferencing from his office. He uses the same capability, along with a shared electronic work environment, to collaborate with colleagues at other universities without having to leave campus. He and his colleagues can even manage experiments at remote locations from their respective offices.

Professor Land has been relieved of much of the clerical work of managing his communications with both the university and his individual students. He is provided with an electronic grade book that he can use throughout the semester. He can use the underlying directory service to establish automated e-mail contacts, chat rooms, and distribution lists to facilitate his providing additional resources directly to students. He can handle students' routine requests electronically, giving him more time to spend with them in person discussing academics, career goals, and strategies. As an adviser, he has access to information tools that give him more detailed information about the performance of his advisees. He can create models of different academic approaches to career goals to help the student understand alternative course paths. By setting minimum performance standards at various milestone points in the semester, his grade book can trigger messages to students falling below acceptable levels to advise them to see him or to refer them to remedial help sources on campus. At the end of the semester, a simple upload procedure moves his grades to the official record of the student.

One could imagine similar scenarios for senior administrators, staff members, alumni, prospective students or employers, and institutional donors.

Themes Gleaned from the Scenario

- Technology supporting the enterprise, not driving the enterprise

  It is key to recognize that although change is being facilitated by various technologies and technology-based services, the best technologies are those that are transparent to the user. If it is really good, the user will not notice it.

- Mobility and ubiquitous communication

  The mantra "anytime and anyplace" has been with us for a decade. On the modern campus, it will be fully realized. Although most staff and administrators will still work out of identified locations at largely identified times, this will be less true of faculty, and students will be truly peripatetic.

- Interconnectedness

  A technically minded person might focus on the network capabilities evinced in the scenario. In terms of campus effect, the important thing is not the technology but what it allows: connectedness. People can be connected to people in ways that allow ideas to flow—from faculty member to student, from student to student, and from student to faculty member. To return to the first sentence of this chapter, connectedness is the essence of the modern campus just as it has been of other forms of academic institutions for centuries.

  Another form of connectedness is that represented by the connection between an individual and the institution. On today's campuses, much of that connection is devoted to what is termed *administrivia* in the scenario. In the modern campus, connectedness will be based on meeting mutual needs.

  Administrative interactions between a member of the community and the institution in today's campus environment typically depend on intermediaries—the right person in the right office at the right time getting or accepting the right information. That is an expensive and nonproductive form of connectedness. Many of those institutional interactions can be managed on a self-service approach if the correct technologies are brought to bear. Thus, the modern campus will feature a much more disintermediated approach to managing logistical events. Members of the academic community will spend less time and effort on the academic counterparts of getting cash from the bank, buying gasoline, and shopping and more time and effort on learning.

  Disintermediation does not mean doing away with the need for people. What it does mean is saving person-to-person contacts for high-touch high-quality interactions, not wasting them on routine administrative operations. Not everything will be handled by technologies. There is a role for people helping people, but it is not in dealing with paper or reading screens for someone else.

- Adaptive devices and adaptive environments

  As with the portal technology described previously, the modern campus will feature much more individualized capabilities. Many current higher education processes are industrial-age relics that take an assembly-line approach that implicitly assumes that one size fits all. With past technologies, this has been the efficient way to deal with the scale of our institutions. The modern campus will initially provide tools for individuals to personalize services and information to their own specifications. Over time, this will evolve into devices and environments that learn preferences as they are used. Rather than being passively available, they will proactively sense when a service may be needed and offer it. This could have many faces. An immediate example that can be foreseen regards tutoring. If a student is having trouble learning a concept, a learning management system will sense the difficulty and offer individualized, supplementary tutoring to aid the learner or connect him or her directly to the teacher.

Learning Environment

The previous scenario describes a modern campus that is recognizably derived from today's traditional university campus. The student is of traditional age (18–24) and works on a physical campus. It is important to appreciate that such students form a dwindling minority of all U.S. university students, about half of whom are now 25 years of age and older. They form the most rapidly growing segment of students. Within a couple of decades they may well double in number and thus constitute about three-quarters of a national university student body that will itself be roughly double its present size (currently about fifteen million).

This implies a profound transformation in the meaning of the word *campus*. The modern campus will come to mean the totality of the learning environment provided by a higher education institution, whether situated around a traditional green, leafy quadrangle or somewhere in cyberspace. (The Romans would never recognize it.) Its learners will be everybody the institution connects with teachers, whether they come to an identified location or not. The learning environment must and will continue to be strongly interactive, but the interactions may be at a distance in both space and time. Increasingly, the traditional concept of teacher-centered instruction is giving way to learner-centered environments, with the teacher taking a mentoring role. This will allow more personalized instruction, in effect returning us to the halcyon days of Plato's Academy.

This learning model might be termed the 3 Js model (just in time, just for me, and just the right content), and the associated information model might be termed the 3 Rs model (right information, right time and place, right format).

Technology is breaking down the limitations of time and place, even for traditional classroom-centered learning. Real-world information can be brought into the classroom on demand; the professor's notes can be distributed before and after classroom discussion, thereby changing the character of classroom interactions; and peer-to-peer and student-to-professor communications can take place on an almost continuous basis in and out of class.

Although face-to-face interactions have human interaction advantages, efficiency often requires rigid scheduling, which may not be possible for some learners. Because the classroom can be conceptually broadened, as described earlier, for those learners it may be possible to totally eliminate the physical classroom interaction component of a course by means of IT.

Research Environment

Academic research is an activity strongly differentiated by discipline and by individual researcher. Nevertheless, IT has increasingly transformed the research environment generally. The requirement to travel is being moderated—a researcher is able to access more information, experimental instrumentation, data, and so on from his or her office than ever before. This trend will only continue as truly-high-bandwidth networking with associated quality of service (QoS) becomes pervasively available. (See www.Internet2.edu for the status of such initiatives and their proposed evolution.)

Similarly, collaboration with colleagues at other institutions is becoming easier without the necessity for travel. (It is useful to remember that the World Wide Web was originally invented to serve the collaborative needs of a very small international community of researchers, a couple thousand high-energy physicists.) Desktop videoconferencing, shared applications, shared whiteboards, shared access to data, and shared access to supercomputing resources are becoming prevalent. The implementation of this also requires high bandwidth to the desktop and QoS-capable networking.

Finally, application for and management of grants is more electronic and requires less handwork by individual principal investigators. This perhaps is the service most appreciated by principal investigators, who generally have suffered from the inflexibility and lack of timeliness in traditional campus processes. Figure 1.1 presents some of the large-scale IT components underlying the modern campus, which are also discussed in detail in the following sections.

Network Infrastructure. In essence, the network infrastructure is what is at the heart of this book and is similarly at the heart of all campus technology and services. Although the term *data network* has had many interpretations over the past forty years, it currently is widely accepted as meaning an Internet protocol (IP)–based network. The medium may be fiber, copper, or wireless; it may be accessed via 56-kb modem or directly attached gigabit Ethernet; but all is tied together by IP standards.

Enterprise Data. This used to be the stuff residing on the campus mainframe of interest to an administrative computing group serving a relatively small number of administrators and staff with information needed to manage the institution. Now it is the source data to manage not only the institution but also the distributed electronic environment. In some

Figure 1.1. Components of the Modern Campus.

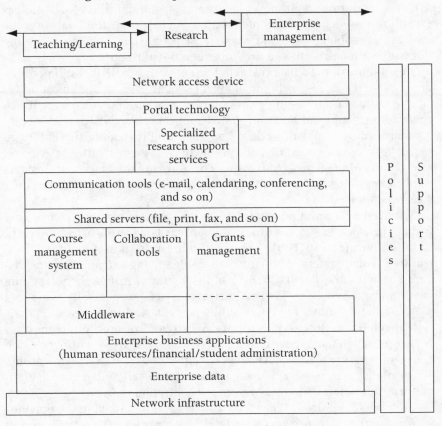

extreme cases, that environment may by itself constitute the modern campus.

Enterprise Applications. These are the applications that manage the enterprise data. In the Modern Campus, they will be self-service, accessed by a pervasive thin client and supporting paperless workflow processes.

Middleware. This is the glue that ties together services and users in a distributed, networked environment. It includes directory services, authentication services, authorization services, and security services. It is based on corporate data and uses accepted or emerging IP standards. Middleware is still a work in progress but will be key to effective use of a distributed environment. Policy decisions will be a significant component of deploying middleware components.

Course Management System. This suite of applications provides the tools for each faculty member to create an on-line learning environment and for students to access that environment. Certainly it will include the ability to put learning materials on-line and manage a class electronically. It will have such capabilities as a grade book that is synchronized with the class roster in the student administration system. It is likely to also have tools for assessing performance. It might incorporate communication tools such as e-mail and asynchronous conferencing. Such applications will become increasingly sophisticated and adaptive, sensing when a student is having difficulty with a concept and providing additional resource materials.

Collaboration Tools. The definition of such a tool set is still not fully developed. At the least it should allow for synchronous communication (as simple as instant messaging or as complex as voice and video over IP). A shared whiteboard and access to shared applications and data are also fairly standard. More sophisticated components might include the ability to jointly manipulate experimental equipment over the network.

Grants Management Software. This is part of the Enterprise Business Application suite but is used only by research universities in support of their research mission.

Shared Servers. Enterprise file-sharing services, printer services, and perhaps network fax services can be accomplished by sharing network servers.

Communication Tools. At a minimum this should include a full-featured e-mail system. Asynchronous conferencing supports on-line discussions with the flavor of in-class discussions. Although not among communication tools, various calendaring services are generally associated with communication services, including personal and enterprise calendars.

Specialized Research Support Services. Research often requires some services that are more cost-effective to provide to the entire research community rather than to have them be duplicated by each research group. This might include specialized applications, large data sets, high-performance computation servers, and visualization tools.

Portal Technology. The portal concept was described in the previous scenario and in actuality is still under development. In fact, at the present time, the word *portal* is used indiscriminately to describe Web pages that bring together links to many other pages or services. The portal concept envisioned in this chapter is much richer than that. At the very least, a portal should be personalizable by each user to allow that user to see just that information or access just those services that are of personal interest. Additionally, rather than being a passive site from which users can go to get some information, a portal should have active elements. As updates to information occur, they should be pushed automatically to the individualized portal access clients of subscribing individuals.

Network Access Device. At one time one might have written "terminal, desktop computer, or workstation" here. All of these still exist and qualify for this role. The diversity of options is increasing rapidly, including the personal digital tablet described in the scenario, but these are only just appearing on the market.

Policies. That this is a complex shared environment is clear. That there are many opportunities for abuse should also be clear. Institutions need policies to make this environment reasonably well regulated, useful, and usable by an academic community. Among the most difficult policy issues on the modern campus will be those surrounding intellectual property. In a learning environment in which it is always easy and usually desirable to share ideas and knowledge, how are we to know what is ours and what belongs to somebody else?

Support. This is perhaps the most critical, and most difficult, component of a campus technology architecture. It takes staff to design, implement, integrate, and maintain all of the components described here—and the myriad of subcomponents not described in this overview. Complementing these staff are those who train the broad community in the use of technology-based services, assist in the use, and are available when things do not work—as eventually will be the case.

Conclusion. The Modern Campus is a learning environment of unprecedented flexibility and effectiveness, provided by an institution that respects and treasures the academic values and traditions of the past while embracing the technological tools that enable it to connect teachers and learners in myriad new ways. Where it is located may not be completely clear (where is the Internet, anyway?), but what it does will touch the minds and hearts of the learners it serves as profoundly as anybody's alma mater ever did. Welcome to the future!

Summary

While some may perceive change in higher education as being measured in geological epochs, the period following World War II has seen enormous change in the nature of higher education in the United States and its impact on society. Thus, although any description of the modern campus is a snapshot in time, much of what now makes a campus modern has been derived from changes resulting from technology, particularly IT in the past three decades. This chapter sets the scene for this volume by describing a current, early-twenty-first-century interpretation of the modern campus with particular focus on the various forms of IT that underlie activities and processes on such a campus.

Reference

Duderstadt, J. J. "A Choice of Transformations for the Twenty-First-Century University." *Chronicle of Higher Education,* 2000, 46(24), B6–B7.

DONALD N. LANGENBERG *is chancellor of the University System of Maryland at Adelphi, Maryland.*

DONALD Z. SPICER *is associate vice chancellor and chief information officer for the University System of Maryland at Adelphi, Maryland.*

2

A better conceptualization of a communication and information system's infrastructure will help campus leaders plan more effectively.

Communication and Information Systems Infrastructure

George R. Maughan

During the last quarter-century, technology has fundamentally transformed U.S. offices, factories, and retail establishments. We have come to understand that if the United States is to maintain its place in the global economy, we must transform our institutions of higher education (IHEs) by infusing technology across the campus. Colleges and universities across the nation have rushed to accomplish this task, resulting in a veritable explosion in the use of technology designed to enhance campus communication and information systems. Unfortunately, all too often insufficient planning has accompanied this expansion. Campuswide initiatives that seek to increase technology use without regard for the functional purposes of that technology take on a life of their own. Scarce resources are wasted, and institutions fail to make meaningful progress.

Regardless of a given IHE's specific nature or orientation, the mission of universities and colleges to pass on knowledge, prepare students for future careers, serve the community at large, and conduct research to solve problems large and small is universal. However noble the purpose, *how* we accomplish our mission—the praxis associated with it—no doubt relates to our success and contributes substantially to how we are perceived within the larger community.

A good source for gaining an understanding the functions of a modern campus is Hanna and Assoc. (2000). The authors focus primarily on the teaching and learning functions of the institution, but they also identify other important campus activities—Philosophy, Mission, Funding, Curricula,

---

Thanks to Gretchen D. Butera for her assistance with this chapter.

Instruction, Faculty, Students, Library, Learning Technology, Physical Facilities, Productivity Outcomes, Governance, and Accreditation—as belonging to the same category of what they call *input measures*. Synthesizing these features along with others, a more general functional analysis of the entire institution renders four primary functions:

1. Academic/Instruction—all aspects of teaching and learning
2. Service/Support—library, printing, housing
3. Management—employees, resources, projects
4. Fiscal—funding, contracts, payroll, tuition

Communication and Information Infrastructures

To function efficiently, IHEs need an integrated, agile, secure, robust, and mature communication and information systems infrastructure. A communication and information system is a set of related parts that function together within an environment to transfer, store and retrieve, and/or process information. A communication and information systems infrastructure is composed of numerous systems. Legacy and new systems coexist with each other to perform various information transfer, storage and retrieval, and processing functions. A communication and information systems infrastructure model is thus a model of variables defining access to information.

In previous decades, specific functions often required specific tools. For example, fiscal units may have required their own software and computer systems to ensure that budgets were managed well. Academic units had their preferences for equipment in computer labs and connectivity. Often these preferences related to curriculum goals. The use of discrete communication and information systems was often related to the familiarity of legacy systems. Contemporary systems offer a convergence of communication and information services along with new or enhanced features that increase access for users.

The layers of technology dedicated to various IHE functions exist in both the traditional horizontal manner, such as optical fiber and wireless systems covering the same geography, and in a vertical integration, where telephone registration systems interface with computers. In addition, literally thousands of software and hardware products are used on campuses, some integrated and some stand-alone. Of course, this layering is, in part, the result of older and newer systems coming into play together.

How well legacy and newer systems are integrated with each other is important to consider. When optimized, systems provide services to different parts of the campus or different services to the same part of the campus. Less effective systems provide redundant or competing nonessential services. As an example, videoconferencing between campuses or business partners has become a popular vehicle for distance education. Often these systems are installed somewhat independently of the existing infrastructure, require separate encoding and decoding devices, and interconnect with transmission cables of radio transmitters. Hardwiring videoconferencing systems to other systems provides advantages because dedicated bandwidth is available, but at the same time, the system may not interconnect with other facilities on campus or at other remote sites.

From this broad view, establishing useful metrics to assess information flow and access is important if difficult. Simple methods are commonplace but tedious and ultimately insufficient, for example, counting words or the number of radio stations in a given area. The data is often difficult to relate to normal communication procedures and can be especially abstract for nonexperts. For example, measuring the rate of information flow by calculating the number of bits per second may not tell the director of student services much about his department's ability to assist students.

Burgeoning communication and information systems have changed the very nature of higher education, allowing information to be transferred, stored, retrieved, and processed by almost all who work, study, or interact with a given institution. Questions associated with who requires what sorts of information, what format of signal is required, and what value should be added are addressed in multiple ways as decisions are made across the institution. If information is the currency of the modern institution, the key to the account is access, which is gained through a communication and information systems infrastructure that is responsive, flexible, and user-friendly.

The convergence of communication and information systems across our campuses has a direct impact on how we frame purpose. Understanding how these systems facilitate the institution's functions is essential. Discrete system analysis has become inappropriate. With the advent of digital systems, more devices can interface with communication and information systems, making the concept of a single-purpose system obsolete. We no longer refer to the telephone system but rather the telecommunications system. Our shift in terminology indicates our consciousness of change. Multipurpose functionality has become the rule in the design of integrated communication and information systems. Not only are systems morphing into one another, but they are also becoming more intelligent, thereby offering more services to users and creating new challenges for campus planners (Baldwin, McVoy, and Steinfield, 1996).

The modern concept of a communication and information systems infrastructure was brought into focus by Masuda (1981) as one of three fundamental components of an information utility. The remaining components that he identified were (1) joint production and shared utilization of information and (2) citizen participation. Of course, he was considering broad applications for an entire society or country, and his view of infrastructure included basic utilities such as electricity and transportation. A far more pragmatic view of a communication and information systems infrastructure appropriate for application to higher education was described in a book that bore almost the exact title as Masuda's, which had been published more than ten years earlier. Dordick and Wang's *The Information Society: A Retrospective View* (1993) devotes an entire chapter to identifying the metrics of their view of a communication and information systems infrastructure necessary for providing access to users for the "production, distribution, and consumption of information" (p. 68).

Any institution that wishes to create an efficient communication and information infrastructure will benefit from a model that can aid in planning, communicating, and decision making (Byrd and Turner, 2000). For example, it might be important to know how Internet videoconferencing, voice calls, and other information services coexist in a technically efficient and cost-effective manner. The value of such an infrastructure model lies in its ability to (1) analyze critical technical and nontechnical factors necessary in making a system work, (2) begin to develop metrics for determining the critical mass of elements, (3) determine patterns of financial resources allocation by function rather than by technical system (in other words, computer), (4) determine impacts of planned upgrades, and (5) create a scalable method of comparing and communicating about communication systems that will relate department- or building-specific access to campus or international systems. By applying such a model to think about coexisting services and cost-effectiveness, new insights can be gained.

A communication and information infrastructure model that includes more than technical devices and networks is essential to assessing how well the communication and information system of a given IHE addresses the functions required. People, money, and policy are essential elements for the following reasons:

- Technical systems are converging and layering.
- New technology and legacy systems often coexist.
- Multifunctional demands are placed on systems designed for single functions.
- Access is essential to accomplishing tasks.
- Communication and information systems are transforming technologies and thus changing the very nature of IHEs.

The Elements of a Communication and Information Infrastructure

Some elements of a communication and information systems infrastructure are regularly recognized as critical measures of how information can be accessed on higher education campuses. Other elements are not acknowledged owing in part to their transparency or the perception that they are not really important. Policies associated with a lab assistant's use of the telephone for personal calls compared with policies spelling out information privacy at the student health clinic may illustrate this difference. And more attention is paid to certain elements of an infrastructure because of technology's seductive, blinking lights, making it difficult to isolate a feature from other roles it may play. For example, the difference between a faculty member's skill at authoring a Web course and her skill at managing that course may appear subtle but can clearly influence to what degree an infrastructure may function.

A robust model of communication and information systems infrastructure includes five major elements, as shown in Figure 2.1: devices, networks, skills, budget, and policy.

- *Devices.* Telephone handsets or headsets, computer terminals, card swipes, fax machines, satellite uplinks or downlinks, videoconferencing cameras, and LCD projectors
- *Networks.* Optical fiber, coaxial cable, twisted-pair copper wire, servers, wireless transceivers, coders and decoders, hubs, bridges, and switches
- *Skills.* Knowledge and abilities to plan, install, maintain, and use components of the infrastructure
- *Budget.* The financial resources to acquire, operate, and maintain systems, including salary, capital, and reoccurring money
- *Policies.* Formal intellectual property, copyright and privacy laws, as well as informal guidelines, rules, and procedures on who, where, how, and when information can be accessed and used, when and how equipment and software will be upgraded and/or replaced, and what type of vendor agreements and partnerships will be established

Creating Access to Information

Access refers to the ability of a user to input or output information that can be processed, stored, retrieved, or transferred. The degree of access to information on higher education campuses depends on the maturity of the communication and information systems infrastructure. Students, faculty, vendors, service providers, administrators, back- and front-office users, and others use information differently. They need to be able to access what they need, when they need it. They should not be able to access information that

Figure 2.1. Model of a Communication and Information Systems Infrastructure

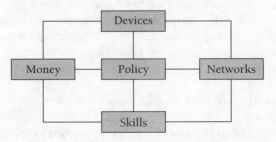

does not pertain to their work or at levels that would enable them to add, delete, or change information.

Assessing an institution's access involves evaluating a number of conditions at the institution. Questions to ask include the following: What type of information format (text, video, voice, data) is accessible? To what degree has value has been added to the information? To what depth may a user probe into a database? To what degree may a user make changes to a file? Certainly, a user must have the ability to speak, type, or otherwise interface with one or many technical device(s). For example, a science student would benefit from value-added data if her computer simulator converted raw numbers to color-coded graphics such as temperature bands that overlay a map of the country and flow into motion to show changing weather over a two-day period. Assessing access allows us to study circumstances such as this. It is important to note that individual media such as data and video were traditionally accessed with separate devices because they required different (data or analog) signal formats and transmission methods. The convergence of systems and the process of enhancing information has changed access in ways that are important to understand.

Infrastructure Maturity

Communication and information system devices, networks, skills, budget, and policy combine to create a whole that is much greater than the individual parts. The behavior of a given infrastructure depends on its maturity. Campuses that have the capacity to originate and receive distance classes featuring two-way audio and video are becoming common. However, if there is conflict about who may use the facility and whether administration meetings take precedence over class meetings or if decisions about using the system for not-for-credit class offerings are made on a case-by-case basis, then the policy surrounding the use of the facility may be problematic. In spite of a mature assemblage of devices, networks, skills and budget, inadequate policies may cause the infrastructure to function at less than its full potential (Kahin, 1993).

It is important to note that infrastructures tend to seek balance. All elements respond to the threshold of the least mature among them—something like the weakest link determining the strength of a chain. For example, when a secretary hand-carries a diskette down the hall to another workstation to avoid going through the procedures to share files on the network, the infrastructure is less than it could be. Or when a financial system of one university unit is not totally compatible with another and it would be more efficient if it were so, the infrastructure is demonstrating immaturity.

In some cases, infrastructure elements can compensate for other elements that operate far below acceptable levels of performance tolerances. For example, when highly skilled computer operators create clever ways to work around a limitation with a local area network, they may be compensating for elements that are prone to failure or have inadequate capacity. The redundancy of some infrastructure elements may be the result of varying levels of subsystem performance. For example, a community college in the Appalachians created a redundant cable-based delivery network for distance education programs when it was found that exceptionally heavy fog in some areas hampered their microwave link with remote sites.

Equilibrium is sometimes influenced by the capacity of individual elements such as servers, switches, and routers, and their capacity is in turn influenced by size. For the most part, larger components are more cost-effective, contributing to the efficiency of the entire infrastructure only inasmuch as the increased capacity is useful in the near term. When considering the element of skills in an infrastructure, the size of a workforce may determine the variety of skill sets available to an institution unit. However, fewer numbers of workers who possess multiple and flexible skill sets may represent or exceed the capacity of a larger workforce.

Equilibrium is a dynamic feature across an entire infrastructure. Fast computers can access the Internet within a range of connection speeds. Yet the true measure of speed is based on the network connection. If the network connection is slow, Internet access may be limited to Web sites without video or animation because these features require a rather large bandwidth. As long as the individual components function at an acceptable level, then maturity may be achieved. As changes are made to an infrastructure, one category of elements may be upgraded while others are not. For example, the once fast computers described earlier may now appear to be slow when the network connections have been upgraded to a very high bandwidth. The entire system may once again work, yet efficiency is now determined by another set of devices. As long as infrastructure elements find some equilibrium within a range of tolerances and there is a critical mass of each element, a relatively high degree of maturity can be established. Those who approach the question of infrastructure efficiency from a purely technical view may consider efficiency in signal integrity and speed. The tendency to separate the technical system components from human, financial, or policy elements may assist troubleshooting a noisy telephone circuit but leaves campus leaders with an inappropriate operational or strategic perspective.

Mature communication and information systems infrastructures demonstrate the following characteristics:

- *A critical mass of each element is evident.* All five categories of elements must contain adequate resources that function within acceptable levels of tolerance, thereby creating equilibrium.
- *Infrastructures are optimally efficient.* When all elements are matched according to the same maturity level, the infrastructure will better accomplish its goals within the institution.

• *Size can be a measure of maturity.* Larger, more complex infrastructures tend to benefit from economies of scale, thereby increasing the potential for efficiency. However, it is possible for smaller infrastructures to be mature.

• *An operational and maintenance plan has been developed and is in place.* Building or expanding the technical elements of an infrastructure may sometimes be easier (albeit more expensive) than maintaining systems. Funds may be acquired for capital investments or ongoing operational funding. In addition, vendors or consultants may or may not be part of an operational or maintenance plan.

• *An ongoing plan to respond to change is in place.* Technology (devices, networks), people (skills), and budget (money) change on higher education campuses. These changes occur naturally in dynamic technological systems. However, thresholds or degrees of change can be anticipated within each category of elements. Priority issues for infrastructure access are critical. Often, differences in perceived needs are based on specific institutional functions of departments. Consistent and constructive communication from all functional units of the institution are critical to keep a focus on their communication infrastructure needs.

Infrastructure Assessment

Communication and information systems are hierarchical in nature primarily due to switching configurations; a building-level (microlevel) as well as a community-level infrastructure will exist simultaneously in an IHE. The interface between microlevel, campus, and community (and larger) infrastructures is often defined by capacity and connectivity. It is possible for different levels of maturity to coexist at different infrastructure microlevels.

Scalability is important to the utility of the infrastructure model because it enables campus leaders to consider changes at one level (building specific) in the same manner as they consider changes in the overall campus infrastructure. The hierarchical nature of communication and information systems is the basis of scaling.

All facilities and buildings have microlevel infrastructures that comprise the same five elements to some degree. It is reasonable to think that all buildings on a campus have telephone service and that all telephones are connected to a switch. The switch may be on campus or nearby, depending on the size of the campus and the relationship with the local telephone service provider. The number of telephones in a building, who has them, the manner through which they are connected to the campus network, the skills of the users, money to pay for service, and so on represent the same categories of elements that are considered on a campuswide scale. When considering similar elements in communication and information systems infrastructures, it is possible to create a more flexible understanding of these elements across site-based and virtual campuses. It is critical to remember that campus services can be extended across the country or across the globe via similar infrastructure components.

Technology Planning for IHEs

Technology planning has become an important part of the modern IHE. The strategic and operational considerations in these plans have resulted in the tremendous growth of information systems and presided over the expenditure of many millions of dollars. The process and goals of such planning have evolved to include many professionals representing numerous departments and interests. This cross-functional planning has big payoffs, especially when the planning process focuses on all infrastructure elements ("AAHE Teaching . . . ," 1995).

Assessing the maturity and quality of a communication and information system infrastructure should be an essential part of an institution's technology plan. The process of planning should be comprehensive and ongoing. Although an institution may engage in an infrastructure assessment and inventory by counting and reporting on the numbers of telephones and computers that exist on campus, this is only a first step. However important in decision making, it typically only covers a few (devices, networks, and budget) of the five major infrastructure elements. If counting is the primary activity involved in planning, the process is limited and fails to achieve an overall sense of how effectively the infrastructure performs throughout the campus. The resulting plan will fail to guide needed change.

In defense of some technology planning, the topics of installation, maintenance, user skills, and legal and operational policies are sometimes considered part of an implementation phase of projects. In such cases, institutions may focus too much on specific projects (in other words, integrating new financial management software), allowing pre-existing skill deficiencies in other areas to remain undetected or undervalued. However, infrastructure analysis may risk focusing on issues that are too broad to be of value. The trick is to ensure that a template for technology planning include both details and big-system or network ideas between and among infrastructure elements (U.S. Department of Commerce, 1996).

One strategy useful in conducting an overall infrastructure assessment is to create multiple teams, each of which is composed of three or four managers from different functional units on campus; a prime example that might facilitate team building would be to recruit them from academic and instruction, service and support, management, and fiscal departments. The team would then perform an analysis of each represented unit by collecting data and considering the communication and information system devices, networks, skills, budget, and policies associated with it. Technical specialist(s) can be made available. Each team would prepare a summary report to be integrated into a campuswide report. This technique has two major advantages. First, cross-functional team members learn a great deal about overall communication and information system features, finding a common language among the nontechnical and technical members. Second, various technology assets are frequently considered in a new light, resulting in a more objective assessment of their campus role(s). In this way, a communication and information systems infrastructure assessment can become part of an institutions' ongoing improvement process.

The following questions may be useful when conducting a communication and information system infrastructure analysis focusing on devices, networks, skills, budget, and policies within an individual campus unit:

- What are the goals and objectives of the unit?
- What is the nature of service or decision making within the unit?
- What is the need for information in providing these services for decision making?
- What are the communication and information system devices, networks, skills, budget, and policies within the unit?
- How do the devices, networks, skills, budget, and policies influence accessing information within the unit and institution as well as outside the institution?
- To what degree do local units have control over their access to the infrastructure?
- What difficulties or problems are encountered with the unit's devices, networks, skills, budget, and policies?
- What future needs and expectations are there for devices, networks, skills, budget, and policies in the unit?

When engaged in future planning for infrastructure development, a technique borrowed from the technical community may be very useful. Owing to the interaction among elements and the overall synergy of a communication and information systems infrastructure, identifying changes and their possible impacts as they cascade through the system is important. Once a baseline of information is established for the devices, networks, skills, budget, and policies of a campus infrastructure, the individual changes (or metrics) in each category could be projected, and impacts on the remaining elements could be forecasted. Taking one change at a time, each forecast would represent an altered infrastructure, sometimes referred to as a first-, second-, or third-level adjustment. By forecasting the changes on all infrastructure elements, a more thorough understanding of future changes can be gained.

Summary

The challenge to integrate technology across campuses provides key stakeholders in the process with an opportunity to improve communication and information systems in higher education. Successfully undertaken, improved communication and information systems will enhance the function of the institution and serve to assist us in achieving the institution's mission.

References

American Association for Higher Education. "AAHE Teaching, Learning, and Technology Roundtable: Improve Education, Use Technology Selectively, Control Cost." *Change,* 1995, 27(2), 48–49.

Baldwin, T. F., McVoy, D. S., and Steinfield, C. *Convergence: Integrating Media, Information & Communication.* Thousands Oaks, Calif.: Sage, 1996.

Byrd, T. A., and Turner, D. E. "Measuring the Flexibility of Information Technology Infrastructure: Exploratory Analysis of a Construct." *Journal of Management Information Systems,* 2000, 17(1), 167–209.

Dordick, H. S., and Wang, G. *The Information Society: A Retrospective View.* Thousand Oaks, Calif.: Sage, 1993.

Hanna, D. E., and Associates. *Higher Education in An Era of Digital Competition: Choices and Challenges.* Madison, Wis.: Atwood, 2000.

Kahin, B. *Building Information Infrastructure: Issues in the Development of the National Research and Education Network.* McGraw-Hill Primis, 1993.

Masuda, Y. *The Information Society as Post-Industrial Society.* Bethesda, Md.: World Future Society, 1981.

U.S. Department of Commerce, National Telecommunications and Information Administration. *Lessons Learned from the Telecommunications and Information Infrastructure Assistance Program.* Washington, D.C.: U.S. Department of Commerce, 1996.

GEORGE R. MAUGHAN is associate professor of technology education and coordinator of the communication and information systems sequence of study at West Virginia University, Morgantown, West Virginia.

3

System planners must understand that user devices serve as a translator between the technology's internal representation of information and what can be perceived, processed, and used by humans.

Information Technology User Devices in Higher Education

Don McLaughlin

Information technology (IT) is a complex mesh of interrelated technologies all working together to perform an information-processing task or meet an information need. A seemingly simple task like sending an e-mail message might involve the use of multiple gigahertz processors, megabytes of memory, gigabyte disk drives, high-speed fiber optics, routers, switches, and so on. Yet most people are indifferent to and only slightly aware of the complex technology that it takes to satisfy our information needs. What they do care about is the user device—the interface between the human user and the information system. It is the user device that allows us to interact with this technology and makes it all useful.

Information systems are very efficient at processing and moving information. However, the machines that make up these systems represent and process information in a form that is very different from anything that would be usable or even recognizable by humans. Computers, telephones, video systems, and other forms of IT represent information internally in a format that makes it processible and transmittable by that particular technology but unusable to the human user. Computers process and communicate information as electronic 1s and 0s, whereas analog devices such as conventional telephone systems move information as electronic waveforms.

User devices serve the role of translator between the technology's internal representation of information and a representation that can be perceived, processed, and used by humans. User access devices convert the 1s and 0s or the analog waveforms into pictures that can be viewed, text that can be read, and sounds that can be heard and understood. Such devices take several forms.

NEW DIRECTIONS FOR HIGHER EDUCATION, no. 115, Fall 2001 © John Wiley & Sons, Inc.

Computers

For years the common lore about the advancement of technology concerned the development of microelectronics and the fabrication of ever-shrinking circuits that could do more and more. Our strides in technology were described in terms of how much more capability a fingernail-sized circuit had than a similar-sized one from the year before. From a human factors standpoint, perhaps a better metric of our advances would be the development of user devices that allows us to exploit the computer technology. Although many people take for granted the devices with which they routinely interact, they can be really appreciated only by knowing that their ancestors consisted primarily of a bank of switches. By setting these switches, the operator could command a computer to perform a well-defined task. These switch settings were, in fact, instructions to the computer but at the most minute level. One array of set switches would be a single instruction, and it would have taken hundreds or thousands of settings to perform anything useful. Such switch consoles would not be considered by most as a user device because access to these switches and the computers they controlled was only available to a very small number of computer professionals.

In practical terms, the first computer-related user devices were keypunch machines for input and the line printer for output. The advent of these devices gave the general user the opportunity for the first time to directly interact with the technology to perform a task or solve a problem. The keypunch machine allowed the user to punch instructions for the computer into a card. Later the cathode ray tube (CRT) terminal was developed. It had the simple job of translating digital data into something we could read and key presses to something the computers can use. This device looked a bit like a modern personal computer (PC) with a video display screen and a keyboard, but it was crude by today's standards. However, it was revolutionary as a user interface device. For the first time people could actually interact, keystroke by keystroke and character by character, with the computer, which, of course, was somewhere else. Even though the computer was a faraway behemoth, you had the sense that you were actually touching it and it was touching you. Also, you could actually back up and correct a mistake, which you could not do with a hole punched in a card. This seemingly trivial feature was profoundly significant. It allowed the user to be more productive and was, it may be argued, the root of modern word processing.

Since the introduction of desktop PCs in the early 1980s, this technology has seen steady but incremental improvement. The 4-Mhz PCs gave way to the 11-MHz PC/AT, which gave way to the 20-MHz PS/2, and so on. With clock speeds of 1.7 GHz, contemporary computers have incomparably better performance than their ancestors of twenty years ago. This trend of faster and faster computers over the past two decades has been correlated with other technology improvements such as higher-capacity storage devices, higher-resolution and faster color displays, and faster communications devices. This evolution of technology was also associated with a corresponding evolution of capabilities, both in terms of what the machines could do and what they enable the human users to do.

The modern PC has become the general-purpose IT user device. They can be found in offices, computer labs, and dormitories worldwide. It seems to be a reasonable wager that the PC is will be the user device of choice for the foreseeable future and for one simple reason—the PC is inherently capable of doing nothing but can be programmed to do just about everything. This does not mean that the PC will not improve. On the contrary, market forces will inevitably drive the technology to even greater performance, more storage, better graphics, and so on. But the PC will remain our primary IT user device for the next ten years or so.

A Laptop in Every Backpack

Although the desktop PC still reigns supreme as the IT user device of choice for most people, the computer has been repackaged in a variety of forms to enhance its portability. The most common form is the laptop, which is, at its core, a PC like all others. Laptops generally run the same software, have QWERTY keyboards, and read diskettes and CDs like their bigger cousins. However, they are being manufactured in small packages weighing only a few pounds and taking the space of a spiral notebook. Their size does not, however, mean that they are less powerful. Although laptops do generally lag behind the desktop PCs on the power curve, they are full-blown computers with all of the capabilities of their desktop counterparts.

Much like computers in general, laptop computers have created a small-scale cultural revolution. Countless laptops can be seen in student unions and libraries. Lecture halls now have power outlets specifically for laptops, and it seems to be more the rule than the exception that speakers at conferences and special seminars bring their own laptops to hook up and use in their presentations. Laptop computers have given rise to the "any time—any where" concept for computing and IT.

Laptops have had a major impact on colleges and universities. A number of IHEs have adopted laptop computer programs, which take several forms. Some colleges and universities buy laptop computers and provide them for each student through a lease arrangement or by raising tuition enough to cover costs. Often the lease cost or tuition premium is inflated somewhat to cover support and software costs as well.

The defining characteristic of most laptop programs is that everyone gets exactly the same computer. This homogenization has a significant payoff for the institution in the form of lower support costs and the confidence that everyone has equal functionality and can run the same software.

Downtime is minimized by simply swapping a broken computer for a working one. The downsides of this approach include, of course, the cost as well as the tendency on the part of the institution to stick with a particular brand or vendor and avoid the migration costs and headaches that would be incurred by switching to a better deal.

The adoption of a campuswide laptop program can add significant costs to both the institution and the student. The *Chronicle of Higher Education* ("Georgia System . . . ," 2001) recently reported that the University System of Georgia discontinued its laptop program due to these costs. In particular, system officials reported that implementing the program in two of its colleges had resulted in a $1.5 million debt for the system as a whole. They believe that they cannot continue to offer these laptops to students at an affordable level and avoid such debt. In fact, eliminating the laptop program allowed these two schools to reduce their technology fees from $300 to $38 per semester.

The recognition that computers are essential tools in higher education is nearly universal among colleges and universities. However, not everyone has adopted the "laptop in every backpack" model. Other colleges and universities had taken other approaches to ensuring that every student has access to needed computer technology. Some, like Virginia Tech, for example, have mandated that students must own a computer when they come to the university but they have left the task of acquiring it to the students or their family and they have not specified exactly what the student should have. These institutions typically define a set of standards or minimal specifications and advise students that if they bring a computer to school that does not meet these specifications, they do so at their own peril.

Another strategy is to refrain from mandatory ownership requirement in the belief that the problem of computer access for students will fix itself. This philosophy has, it seems, been borne out. At West Virginia University, for example, the number of new students bringing a computer to school or buying one after arriving has increased consistently for the past several years. More than 80 percent of new students now bring with their own computer with them. Within the next couple of years it is likely that virtually all students in higher education will have their own computer.

In a sense, students with computers have become a new kind of consumer for colleges and universities and have placed new responsibilities on IHEs. Today's students no longer say "cool" when they find some bit of institutional information on-line; they expect it. Increasingly, students demand to find a course syllabus and course material on-line and are annoyed when it is not there. With equal frequency, colleges and universities are making class registration, fee payment, library access, and a host of other services available on the Web. Failing to do so can place an institution of higher education (IHE) at a serious disadvantage when it comes to competing with other institutions for student enrollment.

Personal Digital Assistants

In some ways the ultimate user device is the personal digital assistant (PDA), also known as the palm computer. These very small devices are designed to fit in a pocket or to be used in the palm of your hand. Unlike laptops, PDAs are not miniature equivalents to desktop PCs. They are functionally less powerful than a PC, although they still possess as much computational power as the PCs of a few years ago.

Most PDAs have a number of fixed functions designed into them. These functions are intended to replace the user's paper calendar or planner, personal telephone book, and notepad, but they often create the impression that the device is limited to these services. To the contrary, most PDAs are, with the correct tools, fully programmable, and a plethora of software for these machines allows them to do a wide range of tasks.

For the most part, the world of PDAs can be divided into two categories based on the operating system that the device runs—Palm OS and Microsoft's Windows for the PocketPC (also known as Windows CE). This almost equates to the PalmPilot and everyone else, but that is not exactly true. In addition to the PalmPilot made by Palm Computing, Palm OS runs on PDAs made by Sony Corporation and by Handspring, Inc. Windows for the PocketPC runs on PDAs marketed by Hewlett-Packard and Compaq.

Perhaps the most important issue about a device's operating system is that it determines the software that can run on the device. Software that was designed to run on the Palm OS for the PalmPilot will probably run on the Handspring Visor (Palm OS) but will not run on the Hewlett-Packard Jornada (Windows for the Pocket PC). This is significant because the software that is available for a given PDA will probably determine the usefulness of that device to a given person or for a given purpose.

Although PDAs have been around for a while, they were slow to be adopted, at least on a large scale. Within the past couple of years they have found widespread acceptance. However, they are still largely used as replacements for paper appointment calendars and rotary index files. Over the next couple of years, we should see a convergence of the PDA, wireless networking, and a broad array of useful PDA software. With this convergence the PDA will likely become a general-purpose information appliance, smaller and more portable but otherwise filling the same function as the PC. It will probably become an indispensable tool for students, faculty, and administrators in higher education.

Telephone

The telephone is perhaps the oldest of the modern IT user devices. It was invented approximately one hundred twenty-five years ago, primarily to enable voice communications between remote parties. Within fifty to seventy-five years of its invention, the telephone became ubiquitous, at least in the United States and to a large extent in the rest of the world.

The traditional telephone is an analog device with a microphone that converts speech or other sounds into electric waveforms, with the strength and frequency of the waveform varying in proportion to the amplitude and pitch of the sound. On the reception side, a speaker receives a waveform from a distant microphone and converts it to sounds. A network of switches and wires connects the telephone sets of two callers through a single circuit end to end. Even though telephones have been around for a long time, the underlying technology upon which they are based remained unchanged for nearly one hundred years. That does not means that they have not changed. Certainly there were improvements in switching systems and in the services available through the telephone line. Fundamentally, though, the residential telephone of today works much like the telephone of the 1920s.

In the 1970s, however, telephone companies began to experiment with equipment based on digital rather than analog technology. Essentially, these telephones receive sounds produced by the human user and convert them to digital bit-streams instead of analog waveforms. The immediate advantage of this for telephony was that the signal could be transmitted as a simpler representation and was less susceptible to noise and interference. The designer of the telephone could define the fidelity of the audio signal and be pretty sure that that is what would be heard on the other end of the telephone call. Ultimately, it would enable telephone companies to develop more sophisticated switching, routing, and control systems for their telephone networks.

Initially, digital telephony experienced only a modest success. Implementing it required not only digital telephone sets for the user but the large-scale replacement of the existing infrastructure as well. This changed with the deployment of the integrated services digital network (ISDN), a fully digital telephony system but with a wrinkle. Recognizing a growing demand by residential and commercial users for access to remote computers and information services along with a limited wiring infrastructure in homes and businesses, the developers of ISDN devised a way to split the bandwidth of the telephone line. That is, engineers were able to take the signal transmission capacity of the standard telephone line and split it into three channels. One channel was assigned to carry standard voice conversations. The other two then were assigned as data channels, each capable of carrying up to sixty-four thousand bits per second of data (less a small amount of telephone control traffic). The typical ISDN telephone looks much like a standard analog telephone except that it has one or two data ports. Through these data ports a user can connect a PC or terminal and dial out to another computer system.

Although ISDN is still widely used in a number of applications, it has never caught on as most people expected, probably because it was just one wave behind the technology tide. Standard ISDN was predicated on the assumption that information users would want slow (by today's standards) terminal-type connections to remote computers. By the time ISDN was in large-scale deployment, Ethernet technology and higher-speed analog modems provided better performance and better access to Gopher and World Wide Web services that were growing in popularity.

The current technology hot topic with respect to telephony is voice-over Internet protocol (VOIP), sometimes referred to IP telephony. VOIP telephone systems are, like ISDN, based on digital technology. However, VOIP telephones are IP-addressable devices and communicate over the Internet or a comparably configured IP-based subnetwork. An IP telephone comes in several forms. In spite of being an IP/Internet-addressable device, an IP telephone can look much like any other office telephone, with the noticeable difference that it plugs into the network outlet instead of the telephone outlet. However, Cisco Systems makes a software product called IP Softphone that enables a standard PC with appropriate microphone input and speaker output to function as an IP telephone. There are even devices that enable a conventional analog telephone to participate in an IP network as an IP telephone.

Like the digital technologies before it, VOIP has not caught on in full force. This is mostly due to the need to replace the telephony infrastructure and the relatively high cost of the equipment. However, VOIP has several important implications for organizations, especially IHEs:

• Most colleges and universities have already invested in new wiring to support their data network. This same network is used by VOIP.
• VOIP allows the institution to be in complete control of telephony deployment. Adding a telephone in a new location is as simple as plugging it in to the data network and configuring it.
• The institution can save money on long-distance voice traffic by routing it to common locations via an IP backbone.
• The institution can manage its own on-campus voice traffic through its data network.

VOIP is probably the wave of the future in voice telephony, partially for the reasons just described but also because it represents an integration of disparate technologies, which seems to be the trend in other technology arenas. However, this prediction will not be realized unless colleges, universities, corporations, and telephone service providers begin to invest in the infrastructure necessary to support it.

People with Disabilities and IT Devices

Up to this point, user devices have been described as the edge of the information system—the place where the information stops. Except for totally autonomous systems, the real end node in an information system is the human user him- or herself. To be effective, an information system must be able to transfer information from the system to the user and must accept information (data, commands, desires, and so on) from the user. The reception of information by the user is ultimately a sensory experience through one or more of the user's sensory organs. On the other side of the process, the emission of information from the user to the system starts as some type of motor performance on the part of the user and must be received and translated by the user device into a form that can be stored and processed by the information system.

User devices such as computers, telephones, video monitors, and the like typically serve the user of the information system well as long as the user's sensory systems are fully functional and the user has the motor capabilities to manipulate the device's input mechanism. However, if users have certain limitations in their sensory systems or in the ability to carry out certain motor tasks, these same user devices can be grossly inadequate or even totally useless.

College and university students, for example, routinely interact with their friends, families, and fellow students through e-mail, chat rooms, and on-line messaging systems. Similarly, the Internet, the World Wide Web, and e-mail have become the preferred means of communicating instructional content and campus information in much of higher education. The central role of technology in education as well as other aspects of daily life is profoundly problematic for people with disabilities; sensory limitations or the impairment of certain motor functions associated with many physical disabilities can render information and IT inaccessible to them. Students with a visual disability, for example, may be effectively cut off from access to critical information that may determine their success in a course.

From a technology standpoint, this poses two major problems for IHEs. First, the institution has a moral, ethical, and legal responsibility to guarantee that every student and faculty member has access to the IT needed to be academically successful. However, the very devices that are designed to provide ready access to information and information resources may be serious barriers to that same information for a person with disabilities. Typically, then, it is incumbent upon the college or university to make adjustments or accommodations that will enable these students to access the academically critical IT.

Fortunately, there are technological solutions to the accessibility problems posed by conventional user devices. Screen reader software such as JAWS enable a visually limited student, for example, to hear and ingest information that is mostly textual and readily available to other students in e-mail, Web pages, and electronic documents. On the input side, a person unable to use a standard keyboard because of a motor disability might use a voice recognition program such as Dragon Naturally Speaking to input the text of a paper, respond to an e-mail message, or browse the Web. A myriad of other software and hardware solutions can turn an inaccessible piece of computer equipment into a productive user device.

Due, in part, to the Americans with Disabilities Act along with other federal legislation and regulations, IHEs are required to ensure that persons with disabilities have equal access to programs and services (Heyward, 1998). This goes beyond the conventional issues of architectural barriers. Given the preeminent role that technology has taken in the education process, colleges and universities must also make sure that their students with disabilities have access to campus computer technology.

Most higher education institutions have dealt with the issue of access to computing technology by students and employees with disabilities, although their programs and approaches vary considerably (Kramer and others, 1989). Probably the most common approach with respect to students with disabilities is the creation and operation of a computer lab specifically for them. In such a computer lab, specialized equipment is provided to work around physical or mental limitations and enable those students who use that technology to be academically productive and hopefully successful. Alternatively, some institutions have provided specialized equipment and technical support in general computing labs. Both approaches seem to work, and each has its proponents.

The Future

Animated cartoons of the 1950s and 1960 revealed to us that era's visions of what life would be like in the year 2000. Quite likely, our most salient impression of these animations is how comically inaccurate they were at predicting the future (which is now). The year 2000 has come and gone; we do not have robots washing the dishes, and no one that we know has that bubble-topped car that drives itself to work while we read the newspaper.

If we focus on the particulars, clearly the fanciful writers and animators of fifty years ago were wrong in their prognostications. However, if we step back a bit and look at what they were saying in a more abstract manner, perhaps they were not wrong at all. That is, certain trends or themes are present in their predictions, and these themes have played out. For example, perhaps the speculators of the 1950s saw a trend toward more automation in everyday life and believed that the devices and machines with which we would deal on an everyday basis would become increasingly intelligent and capable of doing more sophisticated tasks. These predictions have in fact proved to be true.

Indeed, the marketplace in higher education as well as in society in general seems to be defining themes that will determine the direction in which technology will develop. As they unfold, these themes will probably tell us—if we do not dwell on particulars—what the future will be like, perhaps not fifty years from now but certainly over the next ten years or so:

• *Access*. The information consumer has continually demanded easier and better access to information. The Internet, for example, has set a new standard for access to information, and the bar is continually being raised in terms of what users expect. User devices will continue to be developed to capitalize on the availability of information resources and convey them to the consumer.

• *Ubiquity*. The concept of information being available in certain places is gone. Information consumers are increasingly demanding anytime-anywhere access to needed information. Information user devices will be everywhere. We have already seen this somewhat with Web browsers in cell phones and Internet terminals in airports. On the other side of the technology coin, colleges and universities must cater to this anytime-anywhere concept. Institutions that do not make information about their campus, programs, curriculum, and courses available through the Internet, for example, will be left behind and unable to compete.

• *Receding technology*. There will be, for some time, a general-purpose information user device, and for the foreseeable future that will be the PC. However, as the technology becomes more sophisticated, information terminals will shrink away into other devices. Your house will know and be able to tell you (no matter where you are) if you left the garage light on. A dorm room may know if its occupant is ill and summon assistance. These devices will not be sitting around on tables and on the floor. They will become hidden in other equipment that is a regular part of everyday life. The critical question for administrators in higher education then will be, "Do we have the infrastructure to support these smart and interacting devices?"

• *Bandwidth*. To the bane of most technology administrators in higher education, colleges and universities have demonstrated an insatiable appetite for communications bandwidth. This will continue. New services and more communicating devices will increase the pressure to make sure that sufficient bandwidth is available.

• *Convergence*. As stated previously, the PC will continue to reign supreme as the information technology device of choice, as least for the foreseeable future. However, these devices will tend to converge, which will not result in one universal user device but rather in all types of devices including some level of multiple functionality. We have already seen this to some extent with cell phones that include a Web browser and cameras that can send e-mail.

• *Wirelessness*. The demand for ubiquity and ready access to information creates demand for users to be connected without being tethered. Wireless networking is rapidly growing in popularity and will show up in a wide range of devices. Although wireless networking is not a user device itself, it does create the opportunity for new classes of devices that will enable anytime-anywhere information access at levels that are only now being imagined.

It is not clear what user devices will show up on the market tomorrow or the day after. Some will be hits, and others will be misses. However, technology producers generally respond to market forces, and the marketplace seems to be clearly expressing the themes and needs that should shape the future of IT. Technology developers will produce the devices that follow these themes and meet these needs. It will be up to technology leaders in higher education to understand how these devices can be exploited toward positive ends in colleges and universities.

References

"Georgia System Ends Laptop Program with Dept. and Claims of Success." *Chronicle of Higher Education,* June 1, 2001, A27.

Heyward, S. M. *Disability and Higher Education: Guidance for Section 504 and ADA Compliance.* Horsham, Pa.: LRP Publications, 1998.

Kramer, K., and others. *Computers and Students with Disabilities: New Challenges for Higher Education.* Project EASI. Washington, D.C.: U.S. Department of Education, 1989.

DON MCLAUGHLIN *is director of academic computing at West Virginia University, Morgantown, West Virginia.*

Campus leaders must understand the connectivity features and options of modern campus communication and information systems networks to make sound future-oriented decisions.

Networks

George R. Maughan, Karen R. Petitto, Don McLaughlin

The networks connecting the devices that compose a communication and information systems infrastructure provide a pathway through which information is transferred, stored, retrieved, or processed. Connectivity provided by network components can enable users to share information across the hall or across the world. Most information technology (IT) system users are unaware of the components or principles that compose a communication and information system network. However, they are surprisingly sensitive about the speed of Internet and database access, the quality of a wireless voice conversation, or the pixelization of video images in a distance education class. All of these are the results of network configuration and capacity. Devices such as computer terminals, video receivers, antennae, and telephone handsets are interface devices that provide access to networks. In part, devices influence the quality and speed of applications; however, it is the network devices that more profoundly influence network quality. The networks in a communication and information systems infrastructure perform two basic functions: signal transmission and signal switching.

Signal Transmission

A communication and information systems device such as a computer, fax machine, or telephone handset converts keystrokes or speech into an electronic signal suitable for transmission through wires or radio signals when attempting to send information to a destination. The channel itself modifies the signal in ways that may be more or less unpredictable to the receiver, so the receiver must be designed to overcome these modifications and hence to deliver the information to its final destination with as few errors or distortions as possible. This representation applies to all types of systems, whether wired or wireless.

Electronic signals travel through networks in either an analog or digital form. Analog signals are voltages making up a continuous electronic wave. Traditional telephone, radio, and television systems use analog signals. Digital signals are voltages consisting of discrete levels. Computers and related devices use digital signals. Because computers and microprocessors are embedded into more and more communication and information systems, the trend toward digital networks is clear.

Various technical methods are used to optimize the number of signals traveling on a specific channel to reduce the need for an excessive number of wires, cables, or radio channels. Digital signals can be compressed to further maximize the use of a transmission medium to get signals from one place to another. Signals in digital form contribute to the convergence of various systems because they can be used to represent voice, data, or video information. For example, an integrated services digital network (ISDN) telephone can carry a voice conversation and a computer data signal simultaneously on the same line, or a distance learning program can show an integration of PowerPoint frames with text and full-motion video with audio on a single screen owing to the nature of digital signals from computers, video cameras, and microphones. The multimedia distance learning presentation however, would require several regular telephone wires to carry all the necessary information.

Wire-Based Signal Transmission

All wires or cables that carry electronic signals are classified as *transmission media,* some typical examples of which are twisted-pair cable, coaxial cable, and fiber optic cable. Traditionally, wire-based transmission media had the reputation of being low cost, secure, and high speed.

Twisted-pair cable is the multistranded wire used for most residential telephones. This thin copper wire was the foundation of the country's telephone system. Twisted pair is also used to connect computers in a local area network (LAN).

Coaxial cable is often used to connect your home television to the cable network. It is also used on campuses to connect computers and other communication devices. A coaxial cable uses a solid single-wire conductor embedded in a dielectric and covered with insulation or a protective shield. Very high frequency signals pass around the conductor (through the dielectric). The signal capacity of coaxial cable is higher than that of twisted pair.

Optical fiber is a single or bundled glass strand through which light signals pass. Light is generated by lasers or light-emitting diodes to create signals that represent information. The optical fiber is used primarily as trunk lines or infrastructure backbone lines on campuses owing to its very high speed and high capacity.

Wireless Signal Transmission

Two-way and commercial radio have used wireless broadcast signals for more than one hundred years; television, a few decades less. This early use of radio waves was based on sound or images being encoded into analog electronic signals, amplified and adjusted by a transmitter and broadcast through the air from an antenna. The signal is really an embodiment of electromagnetic radiation, or more simply put, a radio wave. Receiving antenna(e) detected the signal and passed it through a receiver and decoder where the electronic signal was reproduced in its original form, whether sound or image. In addition to radio waves for wireless networks, infrared light waves are also used. Although radio, television, and telephone (microwave or cellular) are still used on campuses today, wireless network alternatives to connect computers are increasingly attractive to higher education administrators, faculty, and staff alike.

Wireless local area networks (WLANs) promote the most flexible of all connected environments, allowing users to access printers and servers as well as the Internet from a nontethered computer in settings where the user is most comfortable. There are a number of reasons why institutions of higher education (IHEs) might use wireless networks. The computers they support may be mobile or the construction of the building may not easily accommodate new wiring or the users might often need to quickly and easily reconfigure the layout of a classroom or workspace (McKenzie, 1999). Brick-and-mortar institutions that are creating technology plans must accommodate buildings that were constructed throughout their history, sometimes as much as 200 years ago. Wireless technologies are one component of the technology infrastructure that can turn even the oldest buildings into state-of-the-art technology-rich environments. When hardwiring is a problem, a wireless solution can be installed in a hurry—and make a modern-day hero of the telecom administrator who proposes the fast installation of a network (Harler, 1999).

One of the newest trends in higher education is the marriage of connectivity and mobile computing, a combination that can change the face of higher education. Laptop computers allow students to participate in interactive computer events in a classroom environment. Students must consider these mobile computers integral to the educational process for them to be effective in the classroom. Many colleges and universities are using laptop technology to facilitate communication on their campuses and finding it very effective (Brown, 1999).

Not only does the laptop computer give students an opportunity to participate fully in the classroom, but also the student can then continue that work outside the classroom very efficiently. The portability of the machine allows students to become familiar with one computer and use it for many tasks. The same machine can be used for electronic mail and word processing applications as well as for a variety of specific software applications in the classroom. The computer can serve as an interface among students, between faculty and students, and between the college campus and the global community. Combine the mobile computer with a wireless network, and the teaching and learning process has changed to an anytime-anywhere environment.

However IHEs implement communication and information system initiatives, it is imperative that administrators make strategic decisions regarding the network topology. Many engineers have dedicated their energies to controlling the noise in the wireless channel and to ensure that these wireless channels have an acceptable level of security and safety (Hacacute, 1999; Minoli and Alles, 1996; Varshney and Vetter, 2000). Because of the ever-increasing stability of these systems, WLAN technology is becoming more common on campuses, adding another layer of technology for administrators to consider for deployment.

Wireless communication systems can be used in higher education in two distinct ways. A microwave-based system can allow data transmission facilitated by satellite technology to another school location or to a third party, using wireless in a wide-area network environment (Harler, 1999). More typically, a WLAN, either freestanding or layered with existing wired communication technologies, is installed

Infrared technologies are limited in their range and precise point-to-point topology, making radio technology most common among the available alternatives for campuses. Radio has filled the gap for IHEs that cannot afford the higher-cost satellite alternatives but that have a need for applications and user support that is much more sophisticated than just point-to-point printing or file sharing. The emerging trends in higher education require that networks support many wireless communications services, most commonly personal computers but also pagers, cordless phones, cellular phones, and all kinds of personal communication services.

The introduction of the Institute of Electrical and Electronics Engineers (IEEE) 802.11b standard in the wireless industry in 1998 has changed the way many network designers are thinking about this technology. This standard is the agreed-upon technical protocol for the manufacturing of wireless antennae and computer interface devices and has enabled colleges to offer wireless access to buildings where access would not otherwise have been possible. However, adding a layer of wireless access to an existing wired backbone can make access on a campus virtually seamless.

WLAN products include both access points and network adapter units. The *access point* is a radio-based station that is mounted in a fixed position and connected to a wired local network. The network adapter unit contains a transmitter, receiver, antenna, and a bridge that routes packets to and from the wired network; it provides the data interface to the computer. This unit is available in PCMCIA (Personal Computer Memory Card International Association), and it is installed in the computer so that the computer can contact the access point using radio technology.

The WLAN design has three main considerations in the planning stage: distance, capacity, and cost. The layout must be based on measurements, not just on rule-of-thumb calculations. These measurements involve extensive testing and careful consideration of radio propagation issues when the service area is large, for example, an entire campus. Even a very carefully considered access point layout may have to be modified after installation is complete to remedy coverage gaps. The coverage area of an access point is relatively small, so terrain is not a propagation issue; rather, the layout and construction of buildings determine the coverage area of each access point. Wood, plaster, and glass are not serious barriers to WLAN radio transmissions, but brick and concrete walls can be; the greatest obstacle to radio transmissions commonly found in office environments is metal found in desks, filing cabinets, reinforced concrete, and elevator shafts. The design should also consider the issue of capacity. If many users of mobile computers are located in a small area (for example, students in a classroom or lecture hall), multiple access points may be needed to serve the group. This implies that each access point has a smaller coverage area than might otherwise be possible. The other consideration is application; the designer must consider the types of applications found in the higher education environment and forecast for those that will likely be deployed in a given campus sector.

Signal Switching

Bandwidth provides capacity, like space inside a pipeline, to move information from one place to another. Bandwidth is influenced by the transmission medium (cables, radio signals, fiber) and devices that switch and interconnect devices and systems. It is usually measured by the speed and amount of information traveling through the medium. Bandwidth varies across large systems. On most campuses, bandwidth is the overall currency that influences how many users may access a system; whether text, data, or video can travel through the system; and how fast information will travel through the system. Thus, the functionality of a system is frequently determined by the available bandwidth, which is fundamentally controlled by switching within the communication and information systems infrastructure.

If there were only two computers or two telephones in the world, then the network that enabled them to communicate with each other would be a simple one with a single path linking the device on one end with the device on the other end. Assuming that any one device on a network should be able to communicate with any other device on the network, the network gets more complicated as devices are added. Consider, for example, a network with four computers (each commonly called a *node*), any one of which must be able to transmit to any other. If each computer is directly connected to each of the other computers in the network, the number of links would increase from one in the two-computer network to six for the four-computer network. That is, given four computers named A, B, C, and D, this network arrangement would require the following links—A-B, B-C, C-D, D-A, A-C, and C-B. Taking this a step further, an every-node-to-every-node network with six computers would require fifteen interconnections. The number of connections grows exponentially with the number of nodes in the network.

Clearly, this approach is not a feasible solution for anything but a very small network. For larger networks, this problem is addressed through the use of a switching system that manages the flow of network traffic through the network from one node to another (and sometimes to other nodes).

In a modern network, the data that must be moved from one machine to another is chopped, as it were, into relatively small packets, or *frames*. A frame includes an envelope that contains the data (a piece of an e-mail message, for example) that needs to be transported from one node to another. A frame also carries routing information including the address of the sender of the packet and its destination. A collection of one or more switching devices uses that information to make sure that the frame gets from where it is to where it needs to be.

Not all switching systems function in the same manner. Depending on their application in a network, certain types of switching systems may be more appropriate than others. Generally speaking, switching systems can be classified into the following four categories:

• *Bridges* are typically devices for linking different networks or types of networks and routing data traffic between them. Bridges often act as gatekeepers, keeping local data traffic on the local network and passing only traffic intended for the network to the other side.

• *Routers* act as high-level traffic cops, determining the flow of traffic from one network or subnetwork to another. They are protocol dependent in that some routers can route some protocols but not others.

• *Switches* are low-level devices that route network traffic from machine to machine based on specific device addressing. Typically, switches have a very high level of performance and are used in place of hubs to increase the performance of campus networks.

• *Hubs* (or repeaters) are, in a very real sense, unswitches. That is, their role is to take frames or packets as input and distribute them to their outputs (links to other nodes in the network). The difference is that hubs do no switching. Any data that arrives at an input is propagated to all of its outputs. Every device on an output of the hub receives all of the data coming into it, and it is up to the node device to recognize data that is intended for it and possibly discard or ignore data that is not.

The magic of most modern communication and information systems infrastructure networks in general—and of the Internet in particular—can be found in the switching systems that knit the devices and subnetworks together into a complex network. These switches must be aware of the source and routing information in the frames to see that they get relayed, routed, and ultimately delivered to their intended destination. The term *switch* connotes for many the idea of a relatively simple device that can be set to one or more states or positions. However, network switching devices are far from simple. They are, for the most part, extremely sophisticated devices with a substantial amount of built-in intelligence.

Contemporary switches and routers are capable of detecting a failed link in the network and, if the paths are available, rerouting the traffic through alternate paths in the network. Likewise, they can determine alternate routes to a destination and route the data traffic based on previously defined criteria such as cost or performance. These devices are often capable of filtering data traffic based on its nature. For example, a college or university might wish to block a computer in a residence hall from functioning as a Web server. This would be accomplished through the configuration or control of the switching device. Switches and routers can be used to throttle the bandwidth available to certain segments of the network. Anyone from a campus that has experienced the Napster phenomenon would understand the need to do this.

The selection and use of appropriate switching devices is critical for the design of modern campus networks. Through the use and control of these devices, network administrators and campus technologies can ensure that optimal bandwidth is available to students, faculty, and administrative offices and provide robust services to the campus and the institution's community of users.

Convergence of Networks

Intelligence built into networks makes it easier for them to interconnect various technologies and expand services. These value-added networks are the result of integrating computers and similar devices into standard telephone switches, computer routers, and a class of devices called *gateways*. Telephone features like call forwarding, speed dialing, and voice mail are the result of value-added networks. A new layer of technology is sometimes required to provide these features (Baldwin, McVoy, and Steinfield, 1996).

Perhaps a fundamental aspect of intelligence is the ability to expand network services. For example, being able to retrieve e-mail from your office computer via a cell phone that will then read the messages to you, without lots of existing network or user device equipment having to be replaced, expands communication and information services. In addition, students, faculty, and staff who have wireless access to network resources in the library, cafeteria, and lounges can begin to employ the full power of IT by using these hybrid systems of wireless and wire-based networks (Brown, Burg, and Dominick, 1998). Converged networks are almost exclusively based on digital signals that can be processed by a variety of types of network equipment. Some analog-based systems, such as the traditional telephone system, are integrated into value-added networks through the use of modems and other signal conversion devices.

Network Assessment Variables

The three main assessment variables in wire-based or wireless networking are cost, speed, and reliability. Evaluation guidelines built around these variables should be in place to help determine the advantages and disadvantages of these technologies.

The actual startup costs for networks include design, equipment and software purchase, and installation. (See Chapter Six in this volume.) Ongoing costs include maintenance of the network and user support. Equipment purchases include the wireless access point and antenna. The next cost associated with the wireless network is that of connecting it to the campus LAN. The most cost-effective alternative is to connect the access points to an existing LAN; in some cases colleges may choose to set up a parallel wired network as Carnegie Mellon University has done (Bennington and Bartel, 2001).

Several fixed variables are used to measure the speed of a network. In wireless networks, the most evident measure of speed is the specification of the access points and personal computer cards. The IEEE 802.11b standard for direct sequence spread spectrum at 2.4 GHz frequency is 11 Mb per second. This standard addresses the potential of the equipment. The next variable in the measure of speed is the traffic, the minimum and maximum number of users that are connected to each access point. Attention needs to be given to the placement of access points so as to provide adequate coverage for the typical campus network user. The WLAN technology that this research addresses assumes the existence of a wired campus infrastructure, which introduces other variables into the equation.

In a pure sense, network reliability addresses the ability of the communication system to give the same results in successive trials. The combination provides a wireless communication system with sufficient aggregate bandwidth to handle massive, synchronized movements of mobile computers. Furthermore, the wireless approach supports optimal routing to each mobile computer without requiring modification of the networking software on mobile computers, nonmobile computers, or routers in the existing Internet.

Summary

As more networking options emerge, the case remains strong that IHEs should investigate the needs of the population as the first step in planning the design and topology of the network. Concurrently, a process must be in place for the development, support, and ongoing evaluation and response of a communication and information system network in any IHE. This process should consist of institutional planning, access, staffing, support, and resources. Combined with analysis of network needs and the total evaluation of the network, administrators can begin to make more quantitative decisions about technology deployment on campuses.

References

Baldwin, T. F., McVoy, D. S., and Steinfield, C. *Convergence: Integrating Media, Information and Communication.* Thousands Oaks, Calif.: Sage, 1996.

Bennington, B. J., and Bartel, C. R. "Wireless Andrew: Building A High-Speed, Campus-Wide Wireless Data Network." *Mobile Networks and Applications,* 2001, 6(1), 9–22.

Brown, D. (ed.). *Interactive Learning : Vignettes from America's Most Wired Campuses.* Bolton, Mass.: Anker, 1999.

Brown, D., Burg, J. J., and Dominick, J. L. "A Strategic Plan for Laptop Computing." *Communications of the ACM,* 1998, 41(1), 26–35.

Hacacute, A. "Congestion Control in a Wireless Network." *International Journal of Network Management,* 1999, 9(3), 185–192.

Harler, C. "Colleges Take to the Air." *Journal of Telecommunications in Higher Education,* 1999, 3(4), 12–19.

McKenzie, Ross A. "Wireless Laptop Computing: A New Direction in Student Computing." Paper presented at CUMREC '99, the College and University Information Services Conference, sponsored by Educause, San Antonio, TX, May 9–12, 1999.

Minoli, D., and Alles, A. *LAN, ATM, and LAN Emulation Technologies.* Boston: Artech House, 1996.

Varshney, U., and Vetter, R. "Emerging Mobile and Wireless Networks." *Communications of the ACM,* 2000, 43(6), 73–81.

GEORGE R. MAUGHAN is associate professor of technology education and coordinator of the communication and information systems sequence of study at West Virginia University, Morgantown, West Virginia.

KAREN R. PETITTO is IT specialist and assistant professor of educational technology at West Virginia Wesleyan College in Buckhannon, West Virginia.

DON MCLAUGHLIN is director of academic computing at West Virginia University, Morgantown, West Virginia.

5

Users and managers of information technology need evolving skills as well as an awareness of how changing technology makes them dependent on each other in new ways.

Communication and Information Systems Infrastructure Skills

George R. Maughan

As institutions of higher education (IHEs) strive to improve productivity and reduce costs, the manner by which the communication and information systems infrastructure is built and maintained and how well faculty, staff, administration, and students access it become critical leadership issues. A quick walk around campus will prove that communication and information devices have changed rapidly over the past decade. Changes from telephone answering machines to voice mail, from calculators to computers, from fundamental to exotic programming languages, from mechanical paste-up of printed pages to electronic publishing, from standard overhead to computer projectors, and from cash register keying to scanning as well as the ever-present fax machine are testimony to new this change process. All functional areas of IHEs have undergone change (as outlined in Chapter One of this volume), including new tools to access, transfer, store, retrieve, and process information along with changes in the work performed by (and thus the skills required of) all involved in IHEs.

A large land-grant university may employ thousands of individuals working in more than seven hundred fifty job categories across campus ranging from academic advisor to pharmacy stores supervisor or unemployment compensation specialist. For each employee, the ability to perform the tasks required by each job are influenced by a number of factors: knowledge, experience, complexity and problem-solving capability, freedom of action, scope and effect, intrasystems contacts, external contacts, indirect supervision, and/or physical demands. It is clear that the degree to which individuals access communication and information systems varies greatly, but those systems now influence all IHE environments. Regardless

NEW DIRECTIONS FOR HIGHER EDUCATION, no. 115, Fall 2001 © John Wiley & Sons, Inc.

of their actual job title, many campus employees are knowledge or information workers who are expected to use communications and information provided by technical systems to make the decisions and perform the tasks involved in their job.

When given a choice, most individuals adapt to innovation and change in communication and information systems and integrate these changes into their way of working to varying degrees. Some are early adopters, and some are late adopters; some are unable to adopt innovation, and a few overadopt (Rogers, 1995). Further, most IHEs themselves can be characterized as early adopters and are quick to respond to change, whereas others resist it. When new devices, software, or processes are integrated into communication and information systems in a nearly self-augmenting manner that sustains the importance and evolution of the system, the system has reached a patter of adoption called "critical mass" (Rogers, 1995, p. 313). As these systems evolve, applications within an institution are expanded. Of course, the expanding applications of communication and information systems cause individuals who work with these systems to frequently adjust to change. This means that whether we accept changes as a result of communication and information systems or not, the expanding application of these systems will continue to impact those who work on higher education campuses. Regardless of the degree of adoption or acceptance, the ability of an individual to integrate new skills and ways of working into his or her personal skill and knowledge repertoire depends on a number of factors, mental and physical capacity being important among them.

Three large categories of workers, each of which performs different roles and possesses different skills, are directly associated with and impacted by the IHE communication and information systems infrastructure: the core information technology (IT) workforce, department managers, and information users. Of course, all IHE employees are information users, which is to say that all belong to this third category; the other two categories of employees comprise those who also plan, build, maintain, and/or manage the systems or information flow.

Core IT Workforce

The U.S. Bureau of Labor Statistics considers the following job categories to fall under the rubric of core IT workers: database administrators, systems analysts, computer support specialists, computer engineers, and all other computer scientists (U.S. Department of Commerce, 1999). Computer programmers and technical and managerial workers from the telecommunications sector are also part of this group of employees that possesses and applies the critical knowledge and skills essential for our modern campuses.

The IT workforce, both professional managers and directors as well as hourly staff involved in the development, installation, integration, and maintenance of communication and information systems, tends to focus on the technology rather than the information. This orientation on devices, network hardware, and software can evolve into a narrow agenda of action.

Two employment trends may influence the campus IT workforce in the future The demand for core occupational IT workers in numerous industries will almost double between 1998 and 2008, making it difficult to retain them at institutions of higher education. As well, the demand for IT workers in education will not increase over this time frame (U.S. Department of Commerce, 2000). Thus, the overall numbers of core IT workers in education will stay about the same, reducing the need to expand their numbers of campus IT workers, but keeping these workers on staff while opportunities grow around them may be a problem. This may not be such a big issue owing to the slow growth in IT sectors during 2001. In what has been a traditionally high-turnover employment sector, estimated at 20 percent a few years ago, a large decrease in demand for IT workers has slowed job shifts. Recruiting, retaining, and retraining is likely to be a large staffing concern among IHE leadership (Giunta, 1998). Issues related to outsourcing IT functions may also emerge on some campuses and, if implemented, will directly impact core IT workers.

Department Managers

Management responsibilities and structures for communication and information systems infrastructures vary across IHEs. The tasks of planning, operating, delegating, controlling, and holding individuals accountable for their performance are executed by chief information officers, information system directors, telecommunications directors, and numerous department managers. Horak (1997) has identified some of their management functions as relating to cost, assets, connectivity, process, and security. Generally speaking, managers of communication and information system infrastructures must deliver solutions to faculty, staff, administration, and students.

Aside from the technical aspects of their jobs, managers deal with a variety of issues that have only recently surfaced. The balance between providing robust access while protecting security and privacy is just one issue. Another is the development and marketing of communication and information services as competitive assets for potential students and faculty. Revenue generation is also part of the discussion among IT managers on some campuses. Communication and information systems can contribute to the institution's revenue stream by offering services such as paging, Internet connectivity, long-distance telephone service, and prepaid calling cards.

The 1996 Telecommunications Act has created opportunities as well as restrictions that apply to IT management at IHEs. On a larger scale, distance education systems are becoming an investment to be leveraged in the virtual university market, where commercial projects are aimed at profit. Commercialization efforts often involve multiple organizations. Acquiring and maintaining a big-picture understanding of these variables is essential for managers because they, more than anyone, influence the strategic *and* operational aspects of infrastructure development and growth.

Insightful managers have made it a priority to track efforts to serve disabled faculty, staff, and students through the use of assistive technology in addition to other IT tools. Motivation to do so has come from the Americans with Disabilities Act as well as institution-initiated programs to make adaptive technology available to meet the needs of individuals. By primarily increasing access to communication and information system infrastructures through numerous telephone devices, large-screen computer-viewing software, keyboard modifications, audio and visual aids, and other techniques, the campus as a whole benefits. A number of organizations such as the Job Accommodation Network provide technical support to both people with disabilities and to businesses on how to implement job-site accommodations.

Kann (1999) has investigated strategies for evaluating campus programs to provide computer technology to students with disabilities. She has found that five models for adaptive computer labs are used on campuses and that different criteria can be used to evaluate the effectiveness of these labs based on whether patrons did or did not request accommodation. Campuses commonly use more than one operational model to ensure access to disabled students. Because few campuses integrate communication and information systems in exactly the same way, its not surprising that some respondents called for more standards in serving the needs of this population. This is compounded by the need to evaluate students on a case-by-case basis is seeking an effective accommodation plan. Kann has also reported that participants identified a critical need for administrators and managers to plan strategically for network development to serve this community of communication and information system users.

Communication and information system managers should possess the traditional management skills associated with interpersonal communication (directing, controlling, and assessing) as well as technology skills relevant for distributed information systems (including client-server technology) selection, operation, and maintenance.

The synergy and convergence of these contemporary systems requires managers to also have the ability to differentiate between IT tools and goals. Often, decision makers are influenced by technology product claims, technical specifications, vendors, or competitors to acquire communication and information devices, software, or systems without keeping in focus the big picture: serving the communication and information needs of an expanding community of learners and service providers. From this, a hierarchical breakdown of operational goals and information system performance metrics by academic and/or service unit should be used to determine the appropriateness of tools to accomplish goals. Certainly the potential for new opportunities as a result of new technical capacity must be able to surface.

Cost has always been a concern for managers; however, the revenue-generating aspects of IT systems have become a relatively new feature for managers long schooled in the creation and maintenance of communication and information systems as cost factors. The trend for students to arrive on campus with their own telephones and computer systems has shifted some of the concern from providing hardware and software for individual users to providing connectivity and transmission capacity. Along with this change and the potential for revenue-generating services, managers must rethink the installation of some IT systems or subsystems as an investment for the generation of revenue.

The potential for shared investment and revenue through consortium building and partnering with vendors and other IHEs has never been better. Joint creation and use of communication and information systems will let institutions compete and cooperate in dynamic ways. Access to supercomputing facilities is a good example of this, as is community-campus partnering on cable television or wireless services. Within the institution, team building with technical and nontechnical members has become an essential task for managers associated with communication and information systems on campuses. Along with this important human resource feature is the need for continuous retraining of staff as well as for the manager him- or herself. The need for training itself is not new; what is new is the vital need for a new type of manager training and the need for continuous training.

Finally, managers must understand issues of access and information flow and use in addition to the technical and financial details of their departments. Extending their way of thinking to include immediate events or individual needs and issues of information flow is their new challenge.

Universal Users

Core IT workers share responsibility for creating communication and information systems that provide access and add value to information with users of the systems. Whereas software and network developers focus on the technology, universal users focus on the information and how they interface with distance education systems, record keeping, word processing applications, Internet and Intranet navigation, and other input-output devices and software (see Chapter Nine of this volume).

User skills described in "Learning a Living: A Blueprint for High Performance—A SCANS Report for America 2000" (U.S. Department of Labor, 1992) provide insight into employee skills as they relate to communication and information systems infrastructure. Contemporary skills needed for solid job performance are grounded in basic skills, thinking skills, and personal qualities. In addition to these foundational skills are skills associated with:

• *Resources.* Workers know how to allocate time, money, materials, space, and staff. Everyone from file clerks to faculty senators should be able to analyze the tools they need to do their job and how communication and information tools and systems could improve or extend what they do and how they do it.

• *Interpersonal.* Workers can work on teams, teach, lead, negotiate, and work well with people from culturally diverse backgrounds. This ability to recognize the genuine importance of the true nature of a person's talents and skills is crucial in today's workplace, where flexibility has become an essential commodity. When cross-functional service and faculty committees work on issues associated with IT, new voices about new issues need to be encouraged.

• *Information.* Workers can acquire and evaluate data, organize and maintain files, interpret and communicate, and use computers to process information. In the old days, the physical acts of a job frequently defined an employee's position. Job descriptors such as accounting, teaching, typing, calling, and posting connote action, and we left it at that. This superficial analysis does little to truly convey that the true nature of the work involves information. Only by achieving a new level of understanding about what, how, and when we do something with information will we be able to adjust to change and take advantage of new communication and information systems.

• *Systems.* Workers understand social, organizational, and technological systems; they can monitor and correct performance; and they can design or improve systems. The simplest tasks in the contemporary workplace have known and some unknown effects. It is the latter that can cause inefficiency and problems. Communication and information systems tend to encourage an "out of sight, out of mind" mind-set owing to the electronic nature of information transfer, storage and retrieval, and processing. Training that focuses on the systemic nature of work and information flow improves overall systems understanding. In some cases, job swapping or information flow tracking is also helpful.

• *Technology.* Workers can select equipment and tools, apply technology to specific tasks, and maintain and troubleshoot equipment. The level of sophistication of the technology limits the scale by which individual employees can perform a range of technology skills. For example, community outreach educators may not be able to perform repairs on a malfunctioning portable computer projector, but hopefully they will know that a road trip need not be cancelled owing to the inability to project PowerPoint images. Instead, they know to print the PowerPoint images and have overhead transparencies made, knowing that almost all schools or community meeting places have overhead projectors (U.S. Department of Labor, 1992, p. 3).

Training

Depending on the size of the institution, hundreds of training days per year are typically targeted for developing skills associated with communication and information systems. Existing training efforts have generally evolved from perceived or real needs. Inefficient skill development often occurs when large campus information systems are introduced and slightly inappropriate training is offered to staff. For example, consider a complex financial management system being purchased for a university. The institution chooses not to buy a turnkey system but rather buys only certain modules of the total software package. This is often the case when an institution chooses to replace a generic information-reporting package with one tailored to the institution. As the new system is introduced to users on the campus, scores of office managers and other financial types are trained on the system, but the training is commonly based on vendor materials, including the generic reporting package. When an institution's effort to write its own reporting module falls behind schedule, users are trained on inappropriate procedures. When the new module is finished as the system comes on-line, users are clueless about how to use the tailored reporting module. Retraining is necessary, requiring a new curriculum and new training events. These events are often ineffective in dealing with user frustration and confusion.

"When a person internalizes information to the degree that he or she can make use of it, we call it knowledge" (Devlin, 1999, p. 15). Of course, the phases involved in this process are complex and transparent. Gleaning data from student rosters or financial printouts and mixing it with previously acquired knowledge usually results in meaning or understanding. Some communication and information systems provide raw data, and some add value, thereby shortening the process by mixing previously acquired knowledge with facts. Comparisons of data may show enrollment trends and variances of change over the years. When a data point falls outside of the norm, a user may then begin to use the information to formulate questions such as "Why is this happening?" and " How important is this?" This simple example shows that the transfer, storage and retrieval, and/or processing of information does not lead to automatic decision making but only provides users with the ingredients necessary for decision making. Of course, having access to the right information at the right time in the right format is essential. However, as communication and information systems become more complex, infrastructure access may lead to semi-automated decision support in a real sense.

Staff members must understand their role in the process or flow of work to have a systemic view of the work performed and the communication and information device they use. It is clear that an experienced office manager or secretary who understands that changing a course classroom is different than assigning a room for a new course will not only tolerate a number of computer screens and certain procedural sequences but will also strive to make sure that the process worked properly by checking a master course room assignment schedule after the change was submitted. The ability to know that an individual's work usually begins someplace and goes somewhere else is an illustration of systemic knowledge. By knowing that an "if x, then y" relationship exists and assuming some responsibility for following up on their work, employees can interface better with the campus communication and information systems infrastructure. As infrastructures become more complex, helping all employees understand that the transparency and abstraction associated with information transfer, storage and retrieval, and processing becomes an important training challenge.

Those who acquire, design, or deliver IT training must work in tandem with managers and system developers to ask and answer two fundamental questions: "What do we teach and why?" and "How do we teach and why?" After answering these questions, the training team must establish the objectives of training. An objective statement that is too simple, such as "To use the new software," is insufficient and rarely produces desired results. Skill and knowledge training is best developed or purchased when compared with performance-based objectives in the cognitive domain. This is especially effective when selecting action verbs from a list stratified according to lower-order and higher-order thinking skills. Action verbs are key elements of an objective statement because they describe specifically what the learner can do after the training. For example, to be able to list or identify the major commands of a student record keeping system is quite different than knowing how to apply these commands in a sequence or for specific reports.

Summary

The skills to plan, build, maintain, and use the communication and information infrastructure are very important elements of the modern campus environment. Employee skills that range from equipment repair to the conceptualization of virtual learning communities require strong basic skill sets as well as systems-thinking skills that consider the flow of information in broad terms. The ability to think of new ways to work, study, teach, and manage is a invaluable asset as innovation causes shifts in traditional functional patterns of IHEs.

References

Devlin, K. InfoSense: Turning Information into Knowledge. New York: Freeman, 1999.

Giunta, C. M. "New Approaches for Compensating the Information Technology Knowledge Worker." CUPA Journal, 1998, 49, 1–2, 5–13.

Horak, R. "Telemanagement Software Systems and Service Bureaus: Critical Tools for Complex Networks." ACUTA Journal, 1997, 1, 1.

Kann, C. H. "A Study to Identify Operational Computer Lab Models and to Develop an Instrument to Assist in Evaluating Programs That Provide Computer Technology to Accommodate Needs of Students with Disabilities in Higher Education." Unpublished doctoral dissertation, Technology Education Program, West Virginia University, 1999.

Rogers, E. Diffusion of Innovations. (4th ed.) New York: Free Press, 1995.

U.S. Department of Commerce. "The Digital Workforce." Washington, D.C.: U.S. Department of Commerce, Office of Technology Policy, June 1999.

U.S. Department of Labor. "Learning a Living: A Blueprint for High Performance—A SCANS Report for America 2000." Washington, D.C.: U.S. Department of Labor, Secretary's Commission on Achieving Necessary Skills, 1993.

GEORGE R. MAUGHAN is associate professor of technology education and coordinator of the communication and information systems sequence of study at West Virginia University, Morgantown, West Virginia.

6

The implementation of new information technologies or deployment of new information services pose challenges for budget planners that must be met with a thorough understanding of the nature of communication and information systems infrastructures.

Budget

Laurie G. Antolovic'

Communication and information systems infrastructure, integral parts of what makes up today's modern information technology (IT) environment, require capital and recurring investments. From the wire and cable plants to the Private Branch Exchanges (PBXs), switches, routers, and end-user devices, a stream of funding is required to acquire the technology, operate and maintain it, support its users, and renew or replace it at the end of its useful life.

Communication and information systems are the channels that connect together the various pieces of a campus's IT environment and enable students, faculty, and staff to access the telephone switch, the voice or electronic mail servers, the computers running applications such as student registration or financial systems, the Web servers that give them a gateway to the Internet, the supercomputers that analyze vast amounts of data, and so on. Simply put, without the communication and information systems infrastructure, the power of a college or university's IT environment will not be accessible by its students, faculty, and staff.

As the bridges, tunnels, airways, highways, thoroughfares, roadways, and driveways of the IT environment, communication and information systems must receive as much planning and financial attention as colleges and universities devote to other infrastructure categories. The IT environment is only going to be as good, robust, and accessible as its communication and information systems infrastructure.

Plans and Budgets

Budgets are complex. Like diamonds, they have many facets. They are plans—expectations of deliverables, with revenue spent to achieve specific purposes (Curry and Baroni, 2000, 4–6.) Indeed, budgets embody the

New Directions for Higher Education, no. 115, Fall 2001 © John Wiley & Sons, Inc.

financial translation of plans. They serve as instruments of control, account-ability, and performance measurement. In an ideal world, colleges and uni-versities should have a global view of their entire IT environment. They should have strategic and operational plans that tie together in a coherent manner the different areas of their IT investments.

Budgets for communication and information systems infrastructure should then be the blueprint of a measurable operational plan. They should be the product of a well-thought-out operational plan guided by a compre-hensive long-term institutional IT strategy. Good budgets reflect realistic revenues and expenses grounded in sound business principles that are aligned with institutional policies and goals.

Implementation of new technologies or deployment of new services poses challenges for budget planners. This is especially true in the realm of communication and IT. There is much to learn, the pace of change is rapid, and in many cases there are no precedents for the undertaking at hand. However, as long as one keeps all these considerations in mind, the budget planner can benefit from past experiences. Hence, developing financial and implementation benchmarks from one's previous experiences or one's peer institutions, in conjunction with careful regular monitoring and budget vari-ance analyses, will result in the refinement of budgets over time.

Planning and Budgeting Considerations

There are daunting challenges in planning and budgeting for today's com-munication and information systems. Depending on present levels of invest-ments in these systems, some colleges and universities will find that many of the costs involved will be entirely new items in their budgets. Colleges and universities that are unable to raise tuition and fees will have to find alternative sources of funding. Arguably, communication and information systems are sometimes considered surrogates for institutional quality, and there is growing pressure to keep up with peer institutions. It is therefore important to pay attention to several critical success factors.

Management Expectations. Managing the expectations of college and university leadership is very important. Technology leadership must ensure that college and university leadership is well informed about the transfor-mational power of technology as well as the inherent risks, present and future, associated with planning and budgeting for implementing and man-aging communication and information systems. Technology leadership must always seek the support of college and university leadership when launching major initiatives to discontinue, re-engineer, or implement new services that may have major instructional, research, collaborative, social, and financial implications for students, faculty, and staff.

Customer Expectations. Today's IT consumer tends to expect ever-increasing speed and capacity at no additional cost. In telecommunication systems, this translates to more connections, faster and higher bandwidth, no busy signals, and a richer communications and information environment capable of transmitting voice, data, and video all at once with the legendary reliability and robustness of the traditional telephone system. Technology leadership must take of all this into consideration and ensure that the customers are well informed about existing and future technology directions and their impact on services and budgets.

Financial Models. In a typical college and university environment, the financial models for telecommunications evolved just as separately and distinctly as its voice, data, and video environments did. Traditional telephone services are typically operated as auxiliary services with a 100 percent or 100 percent–plus charge-back financial models. Traditional data or video is either 100 percent supported through mandatory tax assessments or cost allocation or some hybrid financial model. In a converged telecommunications environment, these disparate models will all have to be restructured in a rational and coherent design as e-mail or videoconferencing or voice-over Internet protocol (VOIP) become as commonplace a mode of communication as talking on the telephone.

Financial models should be carefully crafted so that they make good economic sense, are appropriate for the life cycle of a service, are in compliance with externally and internally mandated policies and regulations, and help achieve institutional objectives.

Shorter Technology Cycle. The effect of Moore's law is understandably pervasive in our communications and information systems. Whereas the traditional telephone switch and copper wiring had useful lives of fifteen to twenty years, the doubling of microprocessor capacity every eighteen months has resulted in ever-shortening technology life cycles. Thus, traditional financial models designed to replace or renew PBXs and wire plants every fifteen to twenty years will need to be scaled to meet today's needs. Switches and routers have a life cycle of three to five years. Today's category 3 or older copper wires will need to be replaced to deliver higher network capacity to the end-user equipment. Although category 3 wire is capable of delivering 10 Mb to the desktop (and with some very strict limitations on distance, even 100 Mb), it will have to be replaced with category 5E or newer standards or with optical fiber in order to deliver 100 Mb, 1 GB, or higher to the end-user equipment.

Convergence of Voice, Data, and Video Networks. With any major technological change, colleges and universities need to carefully make decisions to maximize the returns on their investment. With every wave of new technology, there are many costs associated with being early, middle, late, or non-adopters. These costs can be in the form of money, people, time, influence, reputation, and prestige. It is important for the institution to weigh these costs and decide where to position itself on a technology curve. This is true for telecommunications convergence. Transitioning to convergence technology involves major start-up funding for equipment, the wire and cable plant, end-user devices, transitional staffing, staff training, and the like. In some cases, the use of external consultants may be necessary as well. All of these will need to be planned and included in the budget.

Distance Education. Distance education is not new. Many colleges and universities have had correspondence courses or courses delivered through analog video systems. What is new is the transition to or incorporation of on-line, digital technology such as course management systems that also serve on-campus offerings (Blackboard, WebCT, homegrown systems) videoconferences, chat rooms, electronic mail, course Web pages, digitized library resources, and on-line submission of coursework. There are many new costs associated with this change. The production of course content is no doubt a large element. However, those that affect communication and information systems include the cost of software licensing or in-house development, bandwidth, transmission equipment, servers, and personnel, which will need to be incorporated in the budget.

High-Performance Networks (Internet2 and Beyond). The commodity Internet, sometimes referred to as Internet1, has become so popular that it is now no different from the modern metropolis, with its own set of traffic congestion problems. As such, it is not suitable for the high-performance needs of the education and research community. Internet2 (www.internet2.edu) was founded by a group of universities working in partnership with industry and government to develop and deploy advanced network applications and technologies. Colleges and universities who connect to high-performance networks such as Internet2 will need to budget the costs of membership, connection, and other related expenses.

Wireless Networks. Partly to leapfrog the high cost of wiring buildings and partly to satisfy the desire of users to have network access in informal settings such as study lounges, dining halls, outdoors, and so on, wireless networks are growing in popularity. Colleges and universities that intend to incorporate wireless networks into their communication and information systems must budget for this added cost.

Critical Technical Skills. New technologies require new skills that are highly in demand in the market. Colleges and universities typically cannot compete with corporate-sector compensation levels. Moreover, there is a shortage of critical IT skills.

In its April 2001 report on workforce, the Information Technology Association of America (www.itaa.org) makes the following declaration:

> The demand for IT workers is substantial, although down from last year's forecast. Employers will attempt to fill over 900,000 new IT jobs in 2001. Demand for IT workers is down 44 percent from 2000, a fact no doubt attributable to the slowdown in the high tech sector and the economy in general. The drop in demand does not reflect a fall off in IT employment, which will increase year-to-year. (Information Technology Association of America, 2001, p. 2).

College and university budget planners will need to keep this in mind and ensure that communication and information system budgets provide for ongoing staff training and professional development as well as new initiatives to recruit and retain staff with the critical technical skills required.

The Unknown. Plans and budgets in general should be flexible and include contingencies to handle the unforeseen. In communications and IT, however, one might say that the unknown is the rule and not the exception. Just a decade ago, the commodity Internet and the Web did not exist. Today, they are part of the most powerful, visible, and transformational elements of IT. The technology budget planner must sleep like the duck: with one eye open and half of his or her brain at work.

Elements of the Communication and Information Systems Budget

Revenues. Revenues to support communication and information systems in higher education typically come from a myriad of sources. Many colleges and universities have charge-back models associated with traditional telephone services such as providing dial tone, end-user devices, long-distance calls, cellular phones, and pagers.

Typically, these services are billed monthly or at some other regular interval at rates that are established and guaranteed for a set time period, such as a year. Telephone management systems include robust systems for tracking usage and processing billing. Moreover, faculty, staff, and students find this cost-recovery model intuitive because it mirrors their experiences for similar services that they receive and pay for in their homes. One might think of these services as individual-good services, and one only pays if one requests the service.

In many colleges and universities, telephone dial tone, long-distance resale, paging, and cellular services generate surpluses. The rates are typically set at what the market could bear and not grounded in true economic costing models. The surpluses are used to fund various university initiatives such as building campus data networks, wiring student housing, operating student technology laboratories, and so on. This situation has oftentimes led to strained relationships between the voice and the data communications groups in colleges and universities that have consolidated their voice, data, and video organizations if not their entire array of IT operations. The voice communications group thinks of itself as the moneymaker, the goose that lays the golden egg that subsidizes the data communications group and other college and university initiatives.

With recent changes in federal regulations regarding recharge centers, affected colleges and universities (Office of Management and Budget "OMB" Circular A-21) are subject to more stringent requirements to prove compliance with federal cost-accounting standards. Simply stated, recharge centers must recover only the true cost of providing any given charge-back service. They may not subsidize one charge-back service with revenues from another, for example, dial tone with long-distance resale or data connection with dial tone.

The data network, on the other hand, has typically been supported with funds directly appropriated by colleges and universities. These funds are taken off the top or assessed as mandatory taxes to the schools and service units. Thus, one may view basic data network connectivity as a baseline or common-good service and made universally available to the college or university community without the burden of an entrance or user fee. In some cases, the data network is funded by a combination of mandatory tax assessment and charge-back components. For example, some colleges may charge back a one-time initial connection fee but not for ongoing connectivity and the like.

The video network is sometimes funded in ways similar to the data network. Colleges and universities that run television stations also receive external grants, individual and corporate donations, and program income.

With the convergence of voice, data, and video networks into a common telecommunications system, colleges and universities need to carefully restructure and align these disparate financial models with the new scheme—one in which the technical and service elements could no longer be rationally distinguished from one or the other. In the converged environment, it will not make sense to continue to charge directly for voice service and not for data or video. They are going to be served in whole or in part from a common system.

Because of the fundamental change in the financial model called for by convergence, colleges and universities may find that this is also a good opportunity to thoroughly review their IT financial models. Some have done just that and are using a different set of criteria to design their new models. Examples are determining services that are universal common good, sector good, and individual good. A common practice is to fund universal common-good services through mandatory tax assessments or cost allocations. Sector-good services are those that benefit only a specific sector of the community, such as a school or a service unit. A sound financial model for such service might be a single negotiated charge-back rate for the entire sector. Individual-good services would fit into a per-unit charge-back model.

Expenses

Capital Expenses. Typical elements of a communication and information system infrastructure that require capital costs consist of the wire and cable plant, the PBXs, switches, routers, and servers. The wire and cable plant includes the outside plant, the wire and cable that connect the buildings (interbuilding) and the horizontal and vertical wire and cable from the building wiring closets to the wall plates (intrabuilding.) Also part of capital costs are the environmental systems that ensure the continuous operation of the communication and information systems. The environmental systems include uninterruptible power supply (UPS), heating and cooling systems, fire protection, and security systems.

The fundamental thing to remember about budgeting for communication and information systems capital is that it cannot be considered a one-time investment. This capital investment must have an associated budget of recurring funds for replacement and renewal. The life cycle of the technology must be determined, and the requisite annual life cycle funding must be calculated and set aside. One way of looking at this is to think in terms of depreciation. What is expensed in asset depreciation must be compensated for by setting aside the equivalent amount of cash so that a sufficient level of capital replacement fund is accumulated to pay for the replacement of a piece of technology at the end of its useful life.

If capital acquisition is financed through leasing or credit, life cycle funding can still be ensured if the payments are budgeted as permanently recurring expenses and built into the cost and funding model.

Operating Expenses

PERSONNEL. We need people to plan, design, implement, operate, manage, and monitor our communication and information systems infrastructure. We need technicians and installers, network engineers, service consultants and advisers, support center staff, server system administrators, programmers and analysts, IT security analysts, and management talent. It is a challenge for colleges and universities to compete with the corporate sector for the talent necessary to support its communication and information systems. Higher education typically pays much less for IT talent than the corporate sector. The difference is even more pronounced when the comparison is made on total compensation packages, which may include sign-in bonuses and stock options in the corporate sector. The more contemporary and leading-edge technologies are deployed, the more complex the required technical skills are. In communication and information systems, this challenge will be heightened by the convergence of voice, data, and video networks.

It is imperative that colleges and universities set compensation policies that address this problem. In addition, they need to put in place personnel policies and practices that promote the continued professional development of staff and enable them to nurture and grow internal expertise. External sourcing and the use of consultants should be considered as well, particularly in finite projects that require extensive skills that are not available in-house and not possible to acquire in a short period of time.

BANDWIDTH. The Internet introduced new cost elements to the system, the most significant of which is bandwidth. Bandwidth has become a major cost component of communication and information systems. Internet traffic requires enormous network capacity. Indeed, to many colleges and universities, bandwidth is the single largest cost associated with providing access to the Internet.

The Internet has also spurred increased demand for off-campus remote access to college and university networks. Many colleges and universities maintained a bank of dial-up modem pools to provide remote access to their students, faculty, and staff. Before the advent of the Internet, these dial-up modem pools were used by only a small segment of the population—those who have terminals or personal computers and modems in their homes or other off-campus locations. Primarily, these users accessed campus resources and electronic mail. However, with the advent of the Internet and the increase of computers and modems in the home, the number of users and the duration of each session dramatically increased. Colleges and universities responded to this increased demand by adding more modems and more dial-up lines. To control cost, some also implemented ways to ration usage such as allocating a certain amount of free minutes per user per month and charging for excess usage. Other rationing schemes involve limiting the duration of sessions, especially during peak usage time. Some colleges and universities outsourced their remote access services or negotiated special arrangements with area Internet service providers for their students, faculty, and staff to get individual service subscriptions at discounted prices. Some opted for a combination of internal and external sourcing options. Some also devised ways to generate new revenues to fund remote access such as instituting or increasing student technology fees.

Traditional telephony had trunk lines connecting switches to a central office. The number of trunk lines required could be determined based on the number of telephone lines and the community's calling patterns. This was a stable algorithm until the advent and proliferation of remote access dial-up lines. These users did not fall into the usual pattern. Their calls, which connected them to campus computers or to the Internet, lasted hours instead of minutes. With these long-winded users in the mix, the old algorithm fell by the wayside. Thus, voice communications also saw an increase in cost for trunk lines.

EXPENDABLE EQUIPMENT. End-user devices, whether they are plain old telephones, Internet protocol telephones, wireless devices, desktop computers, or personal digital assistants, need to be budgeted either by the central telecommunications organization, the end user, or both, depending on the financial model. If the telecommunications organization rented out end-user telephone devices to the campus community, then it needs to make sure that its rental rates are sufficient to cover replacement and that funds are set aside to fund replacement. Conversely, if users buy their own telephone devices, then they should be advised to budget and set aside funds to cover replacement.

EQUIPMENT MAINTENANCE AND REPAIR. PBXs, switches, routers, servers, telecommunications management systems, network management and monitoring systems, and environmental systems need to be covered by maintenance agreements to minimize downtime and disruption of services.

SOFTWARE LICENSING AND MAINTENANCE. Software systems typically require up-front initial licensing and annual maintenance costs. Maintenance and upgrades of homegrown systems must also be included in the budget.

MISCELLANEOUS. Running the business of the communications and information systems organization require a myriad of other expenditures.

These include miscellaneous supplies, parts, tools, office expenses, space rental, cost of buying long-distance minutes, cost of outsourcing invoicing, credit card service charges, bank lock-box fees, and so on that also need to be included in the budget

RESEARCH AND DEVELOPMENT. Research and development must be an integral part of a communications and information systems budget. Unfortunately this is oftentimes totally neglected or done on the margin. In today's environment characterized by multiple options and rapid change, it is imperative that research and development based on a new paradigm for IT be carried out to test and gain firsthand experience with emerging technologies. This will enable colleges and universities to have a look over the horizon and have a better view of the opportunities and threats that lie ahead (Mayo, 1995).

COLLEGE AND UNIVERSITY ADMINISTRATIVE OVERHEAD. It is a common practice for colleges and universities to charge auxiliary and service units for their proportionate share of administrative overhead costs. Typically included in administrative overhead is the cost of college and university accounting, purchasing, payroll, human resources, support units specifically set up to serve auxiliary and service units, executive administration, campus security, and the like.

The Future

As Yogi Berra (1999) has said, "The future ain't what it used to be" (p. 119). No other statement better captures the present state and future of communication and IT. The pace of change is so fast it leaves one breathless. It was not long ago that colleges and universities were in crisis mode over a killer application called Napster that zapped every bit of network bandwidth available. The next crisis is just around the corner. That more surprises are to come is guaranteed. For service, technology, and budget planners, the future is full of uncertainty. Financial plans for communication and information systems infrastructures need to be designed to be very flexible, adaptable, and scalable.

References

Berra, Y. *The Yogi Berra Book*. New York: Workman Publishing Co. Inc., 1999.

Curry, J. R. and Baroni, G. J. "Budgeting." In C.M. Grills (ed.) *College and University Business Administration*. (6th ed.) Washington, D.C.: The National Association of College and University Business Officers, 2000.

Information Technology Association of America. "When Can You Start? Building Better Information Technology Skills and Careers." Washington, D.C.: Information Technology Association of America, 2001.

Mayo, J.S. "The Evolution of Information Infrastructures: The Competitive Search for Solutions." In National Academy of Engineering, *Revolution in the U.S. Information Infrastructure*. Washington, D.C.: National Academy Press, 1995.

White House Office of Management and Budget. "Cost Principles for Educational Institutions." Circular A-21. [http://www.whitehouse.gov/omb/circulars/a021.html]. 2000.

LAURIE G. ANTOLOVIC' is finance officer in the Office of the Vice President for Information Technology and chief information officer at Indiana University. She is a major contributor to the implementation plan for the university's Information Technology Strategic Plan.

7

Effective use of new technologies calls for the development of institutional policies in equally new areas of concern.

Higher Education Communication and Information Systems Policy

David L. Eisler

The rapid growth of information technology (IT) and communications networks has created wonderful opportunities for meaningful change in higher education. Linked with these opportunities are significant policy challenges that have multiple implications for access, growth, and innovation. In this rapidly evolving environment, it is critical that higher education institutions develop clear policies for access, content, acceptable and responsible use, privacy, and security for computing technology and network usage. The development of Web-based instruction has created significant new issues in the ownership and copyright of distance-learning materials. With the increase of college e-business efforts, questions surface regarding regulatory issues, financial transactions, security controls, and privacy.

Universities are becoming increasingly dependent on fragile technologies, may have users with limited understanding of the potential impact of their activities, and regularly face potentially destructive forces searching to exploit system weaknesses and vulnerabilities. Given an environment in which legal standards may be ambiguous and usage is increasing rapidly, responsible higher education institutions need to develop and implement policies that establish clear guidelines for university faculty, students, and staff.

Computer and Computer Network Policies

Nearly all campus employees and students now require access to a computer and computer networks. Colleges and universities have become dependent on technology for daily essential operations in administrative processes, communication, scholarship, research, and learning. These technologies must be both reliable and secure. With increased numbers of users and near exponential increases in use, campuses need policies and guidelines that set forth clear expectations and standards for use.

Acceptable and Responsible Use. Part of the educational responsibility for colleges and universities is to educate people in appropriate cyber behavior. Policies regarding acceptable and responsible use cover a variety of other user functions and expectations.

Content. Content is one of the thornier issues for university technology policies. Academic freedom is a tenet of higher education and carries with it expectations for unrestricted access to Internet materials. Although institutions may reserve the right to restrict access, university policies rarely include instances of Internet filtering. One notable exception was the decision by universities during the 2000–01 academic year to restrict access to Napster. Some campuses took this action because of bandwidth concerns or to avoid copyright infringement.

Certain Web materials may be offensive or considered obscene by some. Questions of obscenity bring into play statutes on pornography, indecency, obscenity, and protections of the First Amendment. Although infrequent, the cases most frequently prosecuted involve child pornography and should be conducted with the help of local, state, or federal officials. Care and good legal advice are strongly recommended with these potentially explosive issues.

Web materials posted by members of the university community are potentially accessible to a broad public audience. University policies tend to make clear differentiations between official university pages and personal pages. Some campus policies require personal pages to carry a disclaimer stating that they are not official university documents. Another consideration whether personal pages are contained within the college's domain, for example, college.edu, or placed in a different domain that does not contain the institution's name. Institutions can develop questionnaires to aid in this determination.

Ethics. As in other forms of communication, computer users need to follow university standards regarding discrimination and harassment. The immediacy of computer technology such as e-mail, instant messaging, and discussion postings can encourage users to respond in the emotion of the moment, without reflection. Working at a computer can create a feeling of impersonality in which users may send thoughtless and tasteless items. When carried to an extreme, correspondence can be considered *flaming,* sending a message that may be openly hostile, rude, bigoted, sexist, or obscene.

Fair Use. Fair use is an area of copyright law that allows the public to use materials without obtaining permission and that permits the lending and limited reproduction of these materials. Digital media create the prospect of unlimited reproduction without quality degradation. Some publishers and media companies have responded to this perceived threat by adding encryption devices or attempting to define fair use narrowly. Among many provisions, the Digital Millennium Copyright Act, passed by Congress in 1998, makes it illegal to defeat copyright encryption devices. The Uniform Computer Information Transactions Act, a proposed state law adopted in Maryland and Virginia and under consideration in other states, establishes the validity of so-called shrink-wrap and click-through approaches as a part of contract law. Palattella (2001) presents an excellent explanation of these acts and their potential impact on library services. A thoughtful introduction to broader copyright issues is John Tallman's chapter "Who Owns Knowledge in a Networked World?" in Hanna and others (2000).

Privacy. The government has developed clear federal guidelines and expectations for universities to deal with student data and personal information. With the exception of the financial aid process, most campuses have replaced the use of Social Security numbers with randomly generated student identification numbers accompanied by a personal identification number.

Unlike commercial entities, higher education institutions rarely track or monitor Internet usage or electronic correspondence. Policies preserve the right of colleges and universities to do so on occasion when dealing with complaints or reports of abuse. It is the normal expectation that electronic files will be treated as personal and confidential. Enforcement of more rigid policies, except in cases of clear abuse, can be difficult.

Common Sense and Netiquette. Careful and responsible usage of the Internet can improve efficiency, eliminate wasted time, and avoid unwanted circumstances. Thoughtful users do not respond to every e-mail, copy messages to large groups injudiciously, forward chain mail, or include large files as attachments. Because messages sent via the Internet can be easily duplicated and forwarded, users should avoid sending information they would not want others to read. A commonsense approach is to avoid sending messages that the sender would not like to see published.

Electronic correspondence reflects on the author. A check of grammar and punctuation, as well as the use of a spell checker, should be a part of normal electronic habits. In her *ePolicy Handbook,* Flynn (2001) presents the useful "Netiquette Primer for Employees and Managers." Another excellent source for user guidelines, "Netiquette" (Shea, 1994), includes an online quiz.

Technology Resources. University computing facilities are for educational and university purposes; it is inappropriate to use these university resources for commercial or political purposes. In comparison with policies in industry, universities tend to be more lenient concerning computer use for personal reasons.

The adoption of technology with limited, frequently one-time, funding has created a shortage of key facility resources. Most notable among these are computer labs and technology classrooms. University policies seek to establish guidelines that balance the needs of scheduled classes against open access to computing facilities. Many institutions establish standards for hardware and software that attempt to balance freedom of choice against the need for standardization in terms of support needs.

Policies are designed to ensure that university resources are used for legal, authorized purposes. They prohibit obviously illegal or unauthorized activities such as destruction of equipment, software, and data, duplication of copyrighted materials, the creation or distribution of computer viruses, disruption of services, and the overload of systems. Beyond these policies, guidelines in this area refer to appropriate use in terms of computer time, gaming, disk spaces, printing, or other resources. An excellent example of resource policy is available from the Electronic Frontier Foundation (Rose, 1992).

Access Policies. Access policies establish rights for users, as well as expectations on how those resources will be used. Access normally extends to all members of the university community and may also be provided to prospective students and alumni. Approaches are designed so that users can access information they are permitted to see, but no more than this, and to change information they can change and no more. Users have the basic rights of a fair share of resources. These rights are not transferable to others. Misuse of access privileges impacts on others and in extreme cases can lead to the suspension or revocation of those privileges.

Disabilities. A variety of government acts, including the Telecommunications Act of 1996, extends equal and equitable access to telecommunications. This is one area of federal statute in which policies are reasonably clear. All telecommunications devices and services, including computer equipment, must be fully accessible by individuals with disabilities.

Passwords. University policies govern the protection of passwords to telecommunications resources. Included in these standards may be guidelines on the proper construction and changing of passwords. Clearly, passwords should be protected and not shared.

Home Access. The number of institutions providing dial-up access has steadily declined with the development of commercial service providers. Some institutions maintain policies on appropriate use of this access. The creation of virtual private networks, increased telecommuting, and the access of resources while away from the university will create the need for additional policy work in this area.

Security. Security policies and plans provide for protection from and preparation for electronic and physical threats. Policies concerning electronic threats include data protection, virus detection, preventive practices, and backup systems. In the event of virus infection or compromised systems, policies outline procedures that are to be followed. Campuses should also address physical protection for facility users and procedures in the event of natural or manmade disasters.

Course Copyright. The subject of course copyright has become one of the areas of most interest in information systems policy. Using the Internet and other electronic media, faculty and higher education institutions have created large numbers of Web-based courses. The question of who owns these new courses is an issue of significant confusion and can create contentious and divisive debate on campus.

Copyright Background. Some commonly held misperceptions exist regarding copyright. For example, although a copyright notice may provide some additional benefit, it is not necessary to place such a notice on the work or register it with the U.S. Copyright Office. Copyright protection applies when a work is created. Copyright ownership gives the owner protection and carries with it the responsibility to use that protection. The determination of ownership changes the length of the protection provided: individuals receive protection for the remainder of their life plus fifty years; institutional owners are protected for seventy-five years.

Perhaps most important in respect to courses, copyright does not protect faculty classroom presentations. As noted intellectual-property expert Kenneth Salomon stated, "The fact is: an oral lecture that is not simultaneously recorded in some way, is not copyrightable." Nonetheless, he continues, "Original content that a faculty member develops for inclusion in an electronic course is protectable" ("Owning Thought," 2001, p. 30).

Unfortunately, current copyright law and interpretation make definitive allocation of ownership unclear. Are the on-line courses created by faculty members their property, or do they belong to the university? The answer is that it depends. The issue becomes further clouded if research assistants, graphic designers, or Web designers employed by the university contribute to the project. Three copyright interpretations may apply.

Works-for-hire. Course materials can be classified as work-for-hire, resulting from a determination that faculty created these materials as regular employees of the university. Works-for-hire are the initial ownership of the employer rather than the employee.

Academic exception. Older court opinions based on the 1909 copyright act establish an academic exception, which maintains that most faculty meet the work-for-hire criteria of regular employees but as educators retain their rights in scholarship and other materials. Accordingly, course materials are not classified as works-for-hire. This interpretation is clouded because it does not appear in statute but results from court decisions. Additionally, the 1976 copyright statute supersedes the 1909 copyright act.

Independent contractors. Some course materials, although created by regular faculty, should be considered the work of independent contractors. These course materials are developed as the result of additional payment or release time to the faculty member and are beyond the normal work assignment. Ownership for these works can be mutually determined by the university and faculty and specified by contract.

Ownership Options. From this analysis arise three ownership options. With works-for-hire the university is the copyright owner. Using the academic exception, the faculty member is the copyright owner. Through classification as an independent contractor, either the faculty member or the university could be the owner, which could be specified by contract. In all of these instances the ownership rights could additionally be transferred between the faculty member and university or a third party.

Evolving Approaches: The Unbundling Option. Some believe course copyright should focus less on course ownership and more on the use of the material. This view is reflected in an approach that suggests: "The college or university is not working in its best interest to assert work made for hire; the faculty is not working in its best interest to assert ownership. A far more productive approach is to focus on who needs to do what with a work rather than who needs to own it" (Twigg, 2000, p. 23).

A work group comprising representatives from the California State University, State University of New York, and City of New York systems developed such an unbundling, explaining their approach with the following statement: "An academic environment that best advances knowledge will view copyright ownership as a set of opportunities that may be shared within the university community rather than as an 'all-or-nothing' property concept. . . . [C]opyright should . . . be understood as a divisible bundle of rights that may be allocated among different parties to provide maximum opportunities for sharing and learning" (*Ownership of New Works . . .*, 1997, p. 14).

A Commonsense Approach. Much public attention has been given to high-profile ownership examples. However, such examples tend to be less relevant to the questions on-line education programs must answer, such as: May others teach those materials? If so, under what conditions and to what extent can the content be used? If the professor no longer teaches at the university, may the university continue to use the materials? If the course is developed with university resources, can the faculty member offer the course through other providers? It is important to resolve these questions on campus to encourage faculty to create on-line courses and to ensure that universities have a reliable catalogue of courses to sustain on-line programs. Kenneth Salomon's "Checklist of Issues for Evaluating the Adequacy of Institutional Intellectual Property and Employment Policies and Procedures for Electronic Courseware" (n.d.) is an excellent starting point for campus discussions of this topic.

Telecommunications Policies

University campuses have long-standing policies regarding telephone service and usage. The development of wireless telephone networks and Voice Over Internet Protocol (VOIP) has created new policy challenges in these areas. Issues to be considered include whether the number of service providers and contract options will be limited. Some wireless companies market their services directly to departments with appealing offers, raising the question of how service will be contracted and coordinated on campus. For some campuses telephone systems are profit centers. If university departments or offices choose to replace land-based systems with wireless or VOIP, monetary implications will be attached. One challenge created by phone contracts that purchase time usage per month is the question of payment for personal calls on university wireless phones.

E-Commerce Policies. The development of university e-commerce initiatives includes issues of credit card handling, transaction logging, data encryption, reliability, and privacy. One of the challenges is to allow public access to forms and information but provide protection for university data.

The acceptance and processing of credit cards create potential challenges for the university in terms of privacy and security. Some universities forbid the storing of credit card numbers on university servers, thus eliminating potential problems concerning unauthorized release of user credit card numbers. University policies can limit the amount of transaction data retained and how long they retain such data. Some universities do not permit transaction data to be stored on servers with other data. Policies should specify encryption standards. In addition, a security audit can help identify potential weaknesses in university e-business systems.

Electronic data issues go beyond relationships between the university, faculty or staff member, and student to include data exchange between education providers. Donald Norris notes that the "recently created Postsecondary Electronic Standards Council (PESC) demonstrates the emergence of an association of the key players in electronic commerce in post-secondary education" (Norris and Olson, 1999, p. 37). With increased transfer of credits and the growth of lifelong learning, electronic interactivity among universities is important for the future of higher education.

Policy Development

Change is a constant in the arena of IT policy. The development and adoption of new technologies can render existing policy obsolete and require new policy initiatives. Universities should consider computer policies in the context of existing university policies. When possible, they should reference and draw from extant policies rather than create duplicate standards for information. The goal is to be clear and intelligible when explaining appropriate and inappropriate activities and behaviors. Policies should reference explanations of due process rights and possible sanctions for violators. Additionally, policies should be available and easily accessible for users. Some institutions include the completion of user education as a requirement for network access.

Wada and King (2001) suggest that there are lessons in the formation of effective IT policy, noting that technology is evolving much more quickly than law and business practices and that answers to accompanying policy questions develop more slowly. This environment requires both new policy and constant interpretation of existing policy. As a result IT staff can be placed in the position where they must decide what is appropriate.

Starting Places for Policy Development. Policy development efforts should begin with existing university policies, including the student code, which serves as a contract between the student and the university. The American Library Association Intellectual Freedom Committee's (2000) "Guidelines for the Development and Implementation of Policies, Regulations and Procedures Affecting Access to Library Materials, Services, and Facilities" is a good source of policy recommendations. Hodges and Pavela (1997) provide a thoughtful introduction to creating policies that encourage good practice and respect the rights of others (see Exhibit 7.1).

For examples of other university's policies, Cornell University's Computer Policy and Law Policy List, accessible on-line (http://cuinfo.cornell.edu/CPL/), contains over 500 policies. It is sortable by type of policy, institution, and keyword.

According to Hodges and Worona, computer policies should include six components: "a statement explaining the reason for the policy, a statement about what the policy covers, the individuals covered by the policy, specific examples of inappropriate behavior, instructions about how to report a violation, and information about potential consequences for violations" (1996, p. 5). Effective policies present this information clearly and understandably, without jargon or acronyms.

Policy Development Process. Universities should create policies through an open consultive process, which includes stakeholders. Draft documents should be distributed to campus stakeholders for review and comment and then revised on the basis of this input. Areas of controversy and strong feelings may require multiple revisions. Legal counsel, campus governance organizations, and governing boards should approve revised policies. The policy approval process should include plans for user education, including dissemination and distribution. Policies should be periodically reviewed and assessed for currency, relevancy, and effectiveness. As illustrated in Figure 7.1, this is an iterative process.

Concluding Thoughts

IT has created a revolution of change in higher education. Added opportunities are accompanied by added responsibilities, with the potential for abuse and misuse. Future innovation, content, course delivery, and information access depend on a campus's ability to use these resources wisely and responsibly. As early adopters of communication and information systems, and as education communities committed to the development of the future, colleges and universities should set forth and model best practices of Internet usage, behavior, and civility. These examples should appear not only in the policies created at institutions but also in the educated actions of the society that higher education works to create. Perhaps the late Indian leader and reformer Mahatma Gandhi expressed it best: "We must become the change we want to see."

Exhibit 7.1. Ten Principles of Civility in Cyberspace

Promote Human Dignity.

The Internet is a human institution, designed to enhance the growth and development of human beings. Every person using the Internet should be treated in ways that respect and promote human dignity.

Uphold the Right to Privacy.

Privacy is a component of human dignity. In addition to adhering to pertinent laws and rules, people using the Internet have an ethical responsibility to respect the reasonable privacy expectations of others.

Foster Understanding and Empathy.

Human beings make mistakes and have shortcomings. They are accountable for the harm they do but should be treated with empathy and courtesy.

Know the Limitations of the Medium.

Communication on the Internet is not designed to replicate or replace the full richness and complexity of human interaction. Some direct and subtle attributes of communication are lost in the electronic medium. Anger, hostility, or sarcasm should not be readily assumed or inferred. If such characteristics are evident, they are usually best defused by reason, suasion, and compassion.

Protect Freedom of Expression.

The lawful expression of an idea should not be disrupted or censored. Those who disagree have a better option, enhanced by the power of the Internet itself: The dissemination of a *better* idea.

Respect the Work of Others.

The lawful work of others should not be disrupted, altered, damaged, destroyed, or misappropriated. Nor should the work of others be used without proper attribution. Those who share information on the Internet should state how it might be distributed by others. If there is a doubt, users should ask.

Protect and Preserve Network Resources.

The Internet is supported by values and virtues that promote individual freedom and responsibility, including self-restraint in the interest of others. The resources of the Internet must be protected, enhanced, and shared.

Welcome Newcomers.

The Internet is a forum for democracy. New members should be welcomed, and guided by example.

Discuss and Define Community Standards.

The Internet is a large community composed of many smaller communities. Each community on the Internet has a responsibility to discuss, define and disseminate reasonable standards and protocols for its members. Members of Internet communities have a responsibility to learn, follow, and help improve pertinent community standards and protocols.

Help Mold the Future.

The Internet is uniquely suited to educate, delight, inform, and persuade. Whether the Internet grows in an atmosphere of freedom and responsibility—or is stifled by regulation and acrimony—depends upon the integrity, honesty, diligence, and kindness of those who use it.

Source: Hodges and Parela, 1997. © 1997 College Administration Publications, Inc.

Figure 7.1. Iterative Policy Development Process

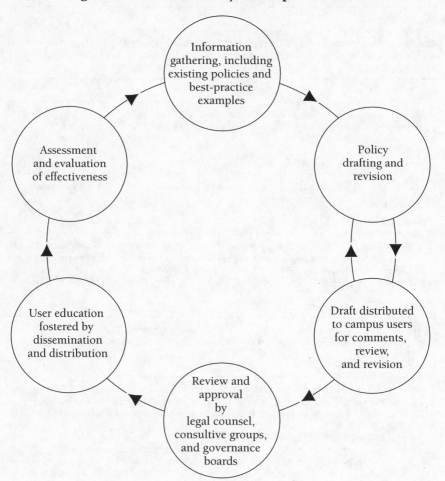

References

American Library Association Intellectual Freedom Committee. "Guidelines for the Development and Implementation of Policies, Regulations, and Procedures Affecting Access to Library Materials, Services, and Facilities." [http://www.ala.org/alaorg/oif/pol_reg.html]. 2000.

Consortium for Educational Technology for University Systems. *Ownership of New Works at the University: Unbundling of Rights and the Pursuit of Higher Learning.* Seal Beach, Calif.: Consortium for Educational Technology for University Systems, 1997.

Flynn, N. L. *The ePolicy Handbook: Designing and Implementing Effective E-Mail, Internet, and Software Policies.* New York: AMACOM, American Management Association, 2001.

Hanna, D. E., and others. *Higher Education in an Era of Digital Competition.* Madison, Wis.: Atwood, 2000.

Hodges, M. L., and Pavela, G. "Ten Principles of Civility in Cyberspace." [http://cuinfo.cornell.edu/CPL/ten_principles.htm]. Sept. 2001.

8

Leadership in guiding the evolution of a college's or university's technology must recognize a context of complex collaborations.

Leadership

Janet K. Poley

As Zuk and Clark (1970, p. 3) noted, "In 1968 Jan Rowan wrote in an editorial for Progressive Architecture magazine that 'surely our present task is to unfreeze architecture—to make it a fluid, vibrating, changeable backdrop for the varied and constantly changing modes of life. An expanding, contracting, pulsating, changing architecture would reflect life as it is today and therefore be part of it. If it is not, rigor mortis is bound to set in.' " Although Rowan was writing about buildings, the idea could just as easily be applied to communication and information infrastructure in higher education today. Educational leaders increasingly recognize that building "stable" information infrastructure is no longer possible and that the mind-set of "legacy" systems always leaves one looking back, not ahead. Information infrastructure must be designed to adapt to change. "We need to work toward processes that will permit a better understanding of the set of pressures on the infrastructure and find techniques that will permit continued evaluation of the pressures and the changes that take place within them" (Zuk and Clark, 1970, p. 9).

The Pressure of Change: Can a System Be Too Stable?

Historically, educators have believed that information infrastructure must be absolutely stable to be good. Tomorrow, success might be judged by how well the infrastructure satisfies the set of pressures acting on it. George Gilder views the entire economy as riddled with time-wasting routines and regimes and believes that the concept of the customer's life span as a crucial and precious resource may define the future of the information economy. In the "telecosm" that Gilder sees on the horizon, the pressures coming from people's limited time will influence the direction of information infrastructure development. He calls the Internet "an unstoppable force that will reach into every nook and crevice of the old economy, tweak it for awhile and then transform it. The Internet saves the customer's time" (Gilder, 2000, p. 250).

Maughan (Chapter Two, this volume) and Hanna (Hanna and others, 2000) clearly describe the functions of higher education today and the elements of the current communication and information technology (CIT) infrastructure. Leadership for appropriate, adaptive, and change-oriented information infrastructure must be shared—there are many actors and many impacted. A commonly understood way for higher education leaders to grab hold of the information infrastructure elephant is still evolving. The old adages about the "blind leading the blind" and the "emperor having no clothes" come easily to mind. In the current context almost nothing is stable. The business of major institutions of higher education is much the same today—teaching, research, and outreach—as it was a century ago. The dramatic change—the pressure—is coming from the increasing demand for learning, discovery, innovation, and convenience. The customer is demanding everywhere, anytime education; rapid real-time research results and applications; global digital libraries; and communication systems that encourage collaboration and relationship building anywhere. The pressure is growing for systems that are at least as good as the old stand-alone stable, reliable operations of a Ma Bell.

Gilder's New Laws

It is a given that the pressure for performance for everyone inside and outside higher education will increase. Gilder (2000)has developed laws pertinent to the communication and information infrastructure of the future. These ten laws challenge the assumption that the building and scaling infrastructure for the future is static or simple:

1. The value of a network grows by the square of the processing power of all the terminals attached to it.
2. Bandwidth grows at least three times faster than computer power.
3. Networks will become black boxes; dumb pipes with intelligence spread to the machines at their peripheries.
4. Bandwidth usability, measured in digital efficiency, grows roughly by the square of the move up spectrum to higher frequencies.
5. Bandwidth is a replacement for power.
6. Fiber trumps copper and the airwaves.
7. The telecosm demands better and better directories.
8. A one-unit decline in bandwidth price yields a five-unit rise in demand.
9. Bandwidth multiplies its own demand.
10. Companies that save their clients time will profit in the telecosm.

Gilder presents ten more commandments, but the point here is not really about his particular view of the future. The point is that it is almost impossible today, and certainly will be impossible tomorrow, to lead in higher education if you cannot understand all the words and concepts in the previous ten statements (or get someone else to explain them to you quickly).

Leading from Inside the Pressure Cooker

Higher education leaders, their faculties, and staffs are in some sense inside the pressure cooker, expected to play an important role in the delivery of a global information infrastructure. Yet on many campuses today, "pretty good Internet" reaches only the chosen few. Simply put, more and better cost money. And because of the tremendous complexity involved in creating "more and better," institutions of higher education are struggling. So are business and industry. Higher education leaders need to have a reasonable understanding of the information infrastructure elements and functions in order to lead. Unfortunately, the real rub comes when the university administrators, deans, directors, department chairs, and faculty are out of sync with their communication and information systems staff. Too often, even when the chief executive officer (CEO) trusts the technical judgments of the chief informations officer (CIO) and staff, they operate from very different leadership dimensions. According to Hanna and others (2000), the CEO leadership wavelength requires

- Knowing the culture
- Reading the context
- Being just in time
- Sharing glory
- Building trust
- Making connections
- Learning from mistakes
- Being accountable
- Building hope and confidence
- Constructing partnerships
- Renewing yourself and others
- Brokering talent
- Using language skills to gain followers

This set of leadership dimensions originally derived not from university presidents but from the successful leadership skills demonstrated by U.S. presidents (not a bad model for pressure-cooker leadership).

Everyone seem to have difficulty determining who is a leader—whether ascribed, appointed, achievement based, and so on. Drucker (1996) keeps it simple. Leaders

- Have followers
- Get results

- Set visible examples
- Recognize that leading is a responsibility

As I have written elsewhere (Poley, 1998), the Internet and networks greatly increase the size and scope of the system that leaders must cope with, and they also accelerate the pace of change within the system. So many in senior leadership posts in higher education are unprepared for what is required in dealing with today's CIT environment. Relationships at all levels are critical, and small changes can have large effects. Leaders must have a complex understanding of everything about the organization—its internal and external environments—and only intervene as appropriate and necessary to stimulate creativity and productivity.

More Pressure: Depth, Breadth, Competence, and Diversity

Bennis and Biederman (1997) note that leaders are often pragmatic dreamers and scientists with poetry in their souls. They liken leaders to maestros, orchestrating congruence toward an attainable vision while ensuring that all contributors are free to do exceptional work. The title of their book in some sense says it all: *Organizing Genius: The Secrets of Creative Collaboration*. The case study in their book that focuses on the development of the atomic bomb is particularly instructive.

The case describes the importance of paying more attention to competence and ability and not to credentials, as well as the importance of analyzing both the human and the technical problems. The situation at Los Alamos also demonstrated a "tragic waste of female talents. Leaders in higher education today cannot afford to waste the talents of anyone, and neither can the lack of diversity in the CIT infrastructure building realm continue to be tolerated. Research continues to show that the lack of inclusion comes as much from unfriendly culture and poor working conditions as it does from anything intrinsic about the activities themselves. It is also important to involve technology users at all stages of the process as the infrastructure is being developed.

CEOs and other senior administrators often experience the most pressure when interfacing with the regents, faculty, legislature, and the university's constituents. Often the pressure focuses on policies, budgets, and accountability questions. Many of the daily complaints, stresses, and strains affecting senior university leaders today are associated with CIT: quality information infrastructure costs too much, it doesn't work, it doesn't reach me, it doesn't support me, it doesn't adapt to my research—and if you don't fix it, we will withdraw our political support, go to another institution, reduce your funding, or make sure you go to another institution. The constantly used mantra that technology is just a tool is likely associated with the desire by senior leaders to reduce the pressures from the human demand system that wants and requires the infrastructure.

Contrasting Leader Orientations and Contexts

Most higher education leaders are gifted at using language to persuade, paint the future, set goals, inspire, console, energize, interpret, and decide. Most excel at understanding people, groups, and cultures and connect easily with how people are feeling. Integrating, comprising, negotiating, and bargaining are primary skills required for survival. Although the CEO may rely on a large number of technical support staff, none are more important than those responsible for budget and fiscal matters. Budget and fiscal competence is simple compared with the complexities required to build a new information infrastructure, and it is increasingly amazing and dismaying that both financial and human resources are inadequately deployed in higher education relative to the responsibilities. The pressure-cooker demands on these staffs are enormous even in terms of attending to the current network demands, let alone doing what is required to plan for and implement future infrastructure aligned with Gilder's coming telecosm.

Too often the CIO and the information system staff receive no support and experience debilitating pressures because of poor and inappropriate decision making by superiors in response to political pressure, underfunding, too little staff, no thanks, daily blame, harassment, and constant challenges to do the impossible yesterday. They are expected to

- Be on top of the future
- Design the new infrastructure
- Support all legacy systems overtly or covertly
- Explain and justify
- Create applications large and small
- Demonstrate cost effectiveness and efficiency

Many who work in the information infrastructure area do so because they enjoy building networks, making things work, and doing things alone. They are often gifted with the ability to see in three dimensions, mentally manipulate abstract objects, and work easily with numbers and code. For things to function few approximations, compromises, or negotiations are allowed. Measurements have to be exact, and code must be correctly written and debugged. The challenge is in the building, and just as cathedrals may take centuries, time may have little intrinsic meaning here. IT workers may view people as an interference. This stands in stark contrast to the verbal political world that other senior higher education leaders function within and manipulate.

Although this description may be somewhat stereotypic, it contains enough truth to underline the importance of consciously incorporating integrators and translators into the system. Even if those involved can agree on the important elements required for building an information infrastructure, that is, devices, networks, skills, budget, and policies (Chapter Two, this volume), the CEO and CIO can unknowingly end up leading in very different directions headed for very different outcomes. In an environment such as higher education, in which lack of time produces tremendous pressure, leaders must put in place the mechanisms to bridge important areas where misunderstandings can impact results. It is important to find the talented people who can bridge the human and technological interfaces and task them with two-way bridging.

To this end small workshops—retreats to which senior higher education leaders, including CEOs, CIOs and their staffs, can come together with futurists, industry leaders, accomplished practitioners, professional associations, and customers—can be helpful. Organizations such as PriceWaterhouseCoopers have fostered this type of session. Such workshops can also result in expanded human networks. Leaders need a broad and diverse set of contacts so they can consult trusted others away from the setting of their own campus. Often on-campus history and politics act as a barrier to quality communication flow. It may be easier for a senior leader to learn from someone who has no ego invested in the situation. Both CEOs and CIOs can benefit from open trusting relationships with opposite types from other institutions. Also, the Web is a wonderful resource that allows leaders to learn quickly what they do not know. Excellent material related to CIT infrastructure decisions can be found quickly through search engines or quality Web pages such as www.adec.edu (the American Distance Education Consortium).

Colleges and Universities Have Many Cultures

Berquist (1992) describes four cultures of the academy: collegial, managerial, developmental, and negotiating. Birnbaum's four types of institutions (1998) are similar and include concepts that help explain life and work in contemporary higher education: the collegial institution, the bureaucratic institution, the political institution, and the anarchical institution.

Although some may find Birnbaum's anarchical institution of higher education chaotic, it appears to be emerging as a stronger and more adaptic form than the other three types. Ironically, increasingly mature and scaled information infrastructure may be at the heart of this type's continued emergence. As Birnbaum explains, "[T]he concepts of organized anarchy are counterintuitive. They defy the common expectations that are part of the more familiar ideas of organizations as communities, as bureaucracies, or as political systems. To understand them requires suspension of some common sense ideas about organizations that we know are correct" (1988, p. 153) According to Birnbaum, rational processes and leadership roles as traditionally viewed do not hold in anarchical institutions. Instead,

Birnbaum explains, three elements define organized anarchy: problematic goals, unclear technology, and fluid participation. Boundaries are easy to cross, and new participants, ideas, technologies and needs are always arriving. Viewing higher education institutions more like a community with questions of leadership considered more as they are in the literature of community development and social change could be useful. Colleges and universities insist on shared governance, with faculty participating with administrators. Looking at leadership from a resource perspective, universities have an abundance of intellectual capital and are short on money. Thus many successful CEOs hold their job predominately because they can bring in dollars. CEOs do this through persuasion, negotiation, and engagement with regents, legislatures, federal government, the business community, and paying customers. Because information infrastructure is expensive, the primary pressure point, which is often brought to boiling, is that between the chief money producer and the chief money consumer. To complicate matters further, colleges and universities are the primary customers for U.S. businesses that make profits through information technology (IT) deployment in higher education. For example, IBM stopped developing a virtual university when it realized that it made much better business sense not to compete with its university customers but rather sell all the infrastructure that institutions needed to compete with each other.

From the discussions of Berquist (1992) and Birnbaum (1988, 1992) concerning the reality of leadership in higher education, the challenges to creating a coherent information infrastructure become apparent. Today's institutions are mixtures of collegial, managerial, and developmental cultures. Historically, the ivory tower is rooted in the collegial culture, meaning that even the CEO is only the first among equals. Because all members have equal standing, the culture is somewhat closed and exists only in loose coupling with its external environment. As Birnbaum (1988, p. 98) notes, "Values that guide the administrative and instructional subsystems . . . are tightly coupled and therefore consistent because of the significant overlap in their personnel. But these same values, such as autonomy and academic freedom, lead to loose coupling within the administrative systems, because giving directives challenges the assumption of equality."

This culture was the prevailing mode before the 1960s, and on most campuses today the senior campus leaders spend considerable time in dialogue with leaders of the faculty senate, deans, and department chairs. From the bureaucratic perspective, which assumes rational organizational behavior, campus culture usually demands that authority is defined by the willingness of the person receiving an order to accept it, rather than the power of the person giving the order. This mode of operation is very unlike that of business and government and results in many meetings and negotiations. Higher education leaders who accomplish things are dogmatic about the ends and flexible about the means to get there. Contingency leadership—that is, if this happens, then we'll get there this way—works well.

Heartburn Happens When Anarchy Meets Structure

Organizationally and culturally, a "structural perspective" implies rationality. A rational organization will have philosophies, goals, and purposes, and leaders of such institutions will assure that strategies, structures, human resources, and technologies are organized, managed, and controlled so that goals and purposes are effectively and efficiently accomplished. The organizing framework for this volume, for example, implies rational structure.

Higher education leaders are unlikely to accomplish the promised potential of new CITs through a structural perspective alone, however. Because higher education is highly political, those involved in bringing a new CIT infrastructure into place most likely will come from the cultural orientations of managing and development. Success depends on complex negotiations among the various cultures. Proceeding on the belief that a "right" solution exists—that one type of device, e-mail system, or product or process must be used—is doomed to failure. In the culture of higher education this type of negotiation goes beyond, for example, the Beta-versus-VHS issue, in which better technology is trumped by a quickly installed base. At its very core the academy will always reject "right" answers. Bright creative people who see that their role in life as finding a better way to do something, discovering the best way to help someone learn, or revealing a fundamentally new truth tend to reject imposed structures or altered structures if they did not participate in the alteration.

Herding People

It is a cultural reality that information infrastructure development in higher education should be accompanied by a major set of process-oriented actions and interventions. Higher education leaders today are just beginning to understand that the introduction of the devices, networks, financial resources, and policy alignments is necessary but not sufficient. They must also deal with the sociocultural aspects required for change to occur.

Some of the most competent and creative information infrastructure developers come from backgrounds in engineering and the military, where the rational organization model prevails. Specialization and efficiency are emphasized, authority is proscribed, and standard operating procedures exist for everything. Although nearly all in higher education agree that a highly robust, ubiquitous, multifunctional informational, and educational research utility is exactly what is required, defining the metrics is difficult.

Most university presidents probably thought there was greater agreement on "What in the World Is Internet2?" than turned out to be the case. In the spirit of "build it and they will come," presidents plunked down their money for bandwidth only to find that once it was built, no one was sure what to do with it—yet (a question of timing, which is always important to

CEOs). The total effects of this growing information infrastructure on higher education and the world are still unclear. And lest we imagine that the thinking about this is all new, Vannevar Bush noted in 1945 that "the world has arrived at an age of cheap complex devices of great reliability; and something is bound to come of it." The world is already glimpsing the good, the bad, and the unanticipated. It will take collaborative work and shared leadership to build an infrastructure that can really make a difference in people's lives.

Leaders Concentrate on Learning the Broad Ramifications of the Infrastructure

Given the importance of this infrastructure to the U.S. and global economies, one will no longer be able to lead institutions of higher education from the top, below, or in the middle without a basic understanding of its far-reaching ramifications. Future faculty will use this infrastructure not just for mail, Web, and word processing but will require the devices, utilities, and interfaces for the fundamental tasks of the academy—teaching, research, and extension. Scientists from many disciplines must increasingly be able to communicate across and through disciplinary boundaries as they discover the impacts of the infrastructure on the economy, productivity, business, commerce, banking, governance, government and citizenship, community, conflict, education, digital libraries, research-knowledge creation, income, employment, and home and family life.

In 1998 the National Science Foundation sponsored a National Research Council (NRC) study of research needed on the economic and social effects of information technology. Although not all-inclusive, the following list is suggestive of some of the broader research challenges that institutions of higher education will require the infrastructure to address:

- Interdisciplinary studies of information indicators
  Interconnectivity index
  Information quality-of-life index
  Leading information indicators to predict growth of the infrastructure
  Home media index
  Marginalization index
- Effects of IT on labor-market structure
- IT productivity and its relationship to work practices and organization structures (considerable evidence suggests that IT's effect on productivity depends on how it is used in organizations, including higher education)
- Intellectual property issues (policy implications)
- Social issues addressed at the protocol level (including how the widespread use of the Internet affects not just intellectual property rights but privacy protection, security, and data filtering)

Leading Cybernetically

Birnbaum (1988) suggests that the cybernetic institution of higher education will provide direction through self-regulation. One reason it is important for higher education leaders, including presidents, to learn more about information infrastructure is because it is increasingly becoming the nervous system, lifeline, and creative workhorse of the institution. Just see what happens when the network goes down. Although it is still early in this infrastructure revolution—particularly with respect to its ability to function as a utility—we are now able to glimpse the many ramifications it will have. Birnbaum argues that university presidents should cultivate leaders from throughout the various subunits of the institution because leadership is not a matter of president's deciding upon a university's goals and then directing people toward goal achievement. In many senses the president's role is more about orchestrating congruence, assuring that resource needs are met, and removing barriers and influencing constraints that impede life in the community.

Symbolic Leadership Is Important

Leaders cannot really change things much directly, but how they deal with the symbolic systems can be critical. "All the world's a stage," and higher education leaders need to be out there on the stage—not in a closet—in order to have symbolic impact. Today, that stage is still largely real, rather than virtual, but one can imagine that as the infrastructure develops, integration of devices, networks, money, people, and policies improve—things don't just go out from the university, but lot's comes back in "real-time-research collaboratories" emerge. The library will then be digital, and global and educational opportunity will be truly available to everyone on the planet anywhere and anytime, in an appropriate and understandable way and at an affordable price. All the world becomes a university, and the concept of leadership shifts. The information infrastructure of the future will be judged by how well it supports human relationships, knowledge discovery, integration and dissemination, and a secure and quality life for all. There is no more important, or greater, leadership challenge facing the world today than to build the right infrastructure for tomorrow.

References

Bennis, W., and Biederman, P. *Organizing Genius: The Secrets of Creative Collaboration.* Reading, Mass.: Addison Wesley, 1997.

Berquist, W. H. *The Four Cultures of the Academy.* San Francisco: Jossey-Bass, 1992.

Birnbaum, R. *How Colleges Work.* San Francisco: Jossey-Bass, 1988.

Birnbaum, R. *How Academic Leadership Works.* San Francisco: Jossey-Bass, 1992.

Bush, V. "As We May Think." *The Atlantic Monthly,* 1945, *176*(1), 101–108.

Drucker, P. "The Leader of the Future." In F. Hesselbein, M. Goldsmith, and R. Beckhard (eds.), *The Leader of the Future.* San Francisco: Jossey-Bass, 1996.

Gilder, G. *Telecosm: How Infinite Bandwidth Will Revolutionize Our World.* New York: Simon and Schuster, 2000.

Hanna, D. E., and others. *Higher Education in an Era of Digital Competition.* Madison, Wis.: Atwood, 2000.

National Science Foundation. "Indicators Science and Engineering 2000." [www.nsf.gov /sbe/srs/seind00/access/intro.htm].

Poley, J. "Creating Shared Leadership Environments in Institutional and International Settings." *American Journal of Distance Education,* 1998, *12*(2), 16–24.

Zuk, W., and Clark, R. H. *Kinetic Architecture.* New York: Van Rostrand Reinhold, 1970.

JANET K. POLEY *is chief executive officer and president of the American Distance Education Consortium, University of Nebraska–Lincoln, Lincoln, Nebraska.*

9

Higher education administrators will need leadership skills appropriate to frequently disruptive but newly empowering technologies.

Changing Practices and New Frontiers

Richard N. Katz

The Communication and Information Systems Infrastructure: A Driver of Change

In making the observation that "the medium is the message," Marshall McLuhan (1964) anticipated the current characterization of communication and information systems (CIS) as potentially disruptive technologies (Christensen, 1997). Profound and rapid changes in technologies often disrupt and even transform the environments in which they are introduced in ways that are both intended and unintended. As McLuhan's work suggests, the medium of communication influences both the form and the nature of communication. Similarly, the nature of the CIS infrastructure is likely to influence and even shape the nature of our higher education institutions and the practices of our faculty and administrators. As Martin Trow describes it, "Information technology (IT) is embedded in, and used by, institutions that have a history. . . . IT will cut its own channels, leading to the creation of institutions that differ from those of today; institutions where the weight of history does not condition and constrain IT's use" (1997, p. 294).

How Is the Communication and Information Systems Infrastructure Model Changing?

To describe or better still, anticipate the influences of the CIS infrastructure on higher education's practices and frontiers, it is useful to summarize some of the key changes to the constituent elements of the CIS infrastructure model.

Devices. With regard to devices, the ongoing driver of change is the continued march of Moore's Law, which posits the doubling of computing processing power at any given price point over a three-year change horizon and has amazing and ongoing implications both for the CIS infrastructure and for higher education frontiers and practices. In technology terms Moore's Law signals the expectation of smaller and more powerful devices and perhaps more important, the imbedding of machine intelligence in all sorts of unexpected devices (Gershenfeld, 1999). Intelligence in Web-enabled telephones is now an expectation. Intelligence in refrigerators, smart cards, windshield wipers, keys, laboratory equipment, books, and other artifacts of daily life are not so well anticipated. Moore's Law also suggests the near-term potential to create devices capable of thought. Today's leading desktop devices approximate reptile brains in processing power. Intelligence of this order is capable of processing multidimensional signals, rudimentary planning, and so on. Networks of thousands of such devices are capable of mastering higher-order activities such as those associated with championship-caliber chess. For students and educators Moore's Law suggests the ready and widespread availability of devices able to support not only the basic-level word processing, spreadsheet, database, and Web browser functions but also devices that support complex simulations, scientific visualizations, multiple media, complex modeling, animation, and so forth. Widespread availability suggests that although there is most certainly a digital divide to overcome, most of the more pernicious and resistant-to-change constraints are likely in the long term to be about educational access and literacy and not about access to hardware.

Networks. Two major phenomena are likely to shape higher education practices and futures in terms of networks. First, Metcalf's Law, which suggests a doubling of bandwidth at constant prices every three years suggests that network-based information and services will be available anywhere and at anytime in the near future. Second, wireless networking will lower both the cost and the complexity of managing "last-mile" connectivity on campus. More important, wireless networking will make it possible for people to stay seamlessly and continuously connected to institutional (and other) networks. In effect, data communications will ultimately enjoy status as a utility, and network connectivity will come to approximate dial tone in availability and accessibility. Governments will increasingly ensure the rights of citizens to network access.

Leadership and Skills. With respect to leadership and skills, MIT's John Rockart (1975) correctly predicted many years ago the bifurcation of the skills that would come to be associated with the CIS infrastructure. He suggested that the technologies would themselves become easier and easier to use through a combination of breakthroughs in both hardware and software engineering. Indeed, the technologies of today's information revolution are reasonably easy to use, reasonably reliable, and perhaps most important, are becoming self-evident to use. Technical transparency has become the design standard of hardware and software systems, aided by the more rapid diffusion of standards through tools such as extensible markup language (XML) and others. Rockart also speculated that at the technical level, the skills needed to develop systems would become more complex. This too has occurred as each generation of semiconductor further erodes the frontiers of physics by fitting more and more semiconductors in small spaces and as software applications demand literally millions of lines of code to operate. The skills required to support the coming wave of progress in robotics, nanotechnology, and other complex areas of development are outside the scope of this discussion. User skills will likely fall into the areas of informational leadership, acceptance of delegation and organizational risk, and innovative use of information.

Informational Leadership. In environments where the CIS infrastructure is plentiful and easy to use, leaders must be able to articulate a vision of the institution that assumes widespread access to information and services via networks. Inherent in such leadership skills are information stewardship, the ability to empower a workforce, and the ability to cultivate "learning" as a core behavior of staff, students, and service consumers in all aspects of their campus life. Information-based organizations also are inherently flat institutions that have been ordered in ways to promote rather than regulate information flows. The very nature of these organizations means that their leaders must be boundary spanners by predisposition and must foster and reward boundary-spanning behaviors within the workplace. Finally, and perhaps most important, the leadership of future information-based organizations will need to be skilled at aligning institutional investments and behaviors in loosely coupled organizational settings.

This is hardly a new higher education leadership skill set. Colleges and universities have been described as *adhocracies,* or as *organized anarchies,* and institutional leadership there has be likened to herding cats. In environments that come to depend increasingly on the CIS infrastructure, alignment assumes new importance. In most colleges and universities IT represents one of the three largest classes of campus expenditures. On research university campuses two-thirds of these expenditures occur in academic or business units outside the direct control of the central campus administration. In information-intensive environments leaders will need to use vision, technical architectures, standards, and incentives to create alignment in this relatively new and rapidly growing area of expense.

Acceptance of Delegation and Organizational Risk and Responsibility. As organizational theorists such as Jay Galbreath (1974) suggest, complex institutions that organize around information require fundamentally different organizational systems and skills than do those organized around decision-making hierarchies. Successful participants in the institutional environments that incorporate a new CIS infrastructure will need to understand how to operate in environments of broad delegations of authority in which access to information and judgment are the coins of the realm.

Innovative Use of Information. Today's knowledge workers in higher education have learned to operate in environments of relative information (or systems) poverty. Decision making in such environments is often political, seeking to satisfice, as Herbert Simon (1965) described, rather than to optimize. In the future technology-enriched environment, colleges and universities will increasingly expect those knowledge workers in their employ to use sophisticated tools and techniques for forecasting demand, revenue, resource use, and pedagogical outcomes. Success in this kind of environment will depend on an intimate knowledge of higher education, the institution, and the information resources and tools that can be invoked to help guide increasingly complex and consequential institutional decisions.

Budgets. With respect to budgets at least two principles emerge as part of the movement toward an advanced CIS infrastructure. First, the infrastructure must be managed more holistically from a budgetary perspective. Although unpredictability and discontinuities are more inherent in IT than in other areas of institutional endeavor, a budgetary model that is rooted in uncertainty and opportunism is not likely to be effective. Central to any contemporary wisdom related to budgets in areas related to the CIS infrastructure is the concept of life-cycle funding. In essence, information systems, like buildings, have one-time costs as well as ongoing costs of operation and maintenance. Like buildings, only more extremely, technologies become obsolete and need to be renewed or replaced. Much of higher education's current chagrin (or worse) associated with Y2K conversion and the replacement of human resource, financial, and student information systems is rooted in its collective failure to organize around the eventual obsolescence of its systems. In environments—competitive and otherwise—that depend more than ever on the CIS infrastructure, the deferral of maintenance on key institutional systems will become increasingly risky and ultimately unsustainable as an institutional strategy and behavior.

Another key principle of budgeting in information-rich environments is to leverage economies and scale and economies of scope. Unlike most areas of institutional endeavor, the CIS infrastructure enjoys the economics of scale and scope. The moves toward thin clients, Web-based delivery, enterprise information portals, data warehousing, and other buzz terms of the Information Age are designed to exploit economies of scale and scope. Budgets should be aligned with standards-setting activities and other strategic investments that seek to leverage scale and scope. Unnecessary heterogeneity in the CIS infrastructure is a driver of both capital costs and other expensive and scarce workforce skills.

Policy. One of the most complex areas of impact associated with the emerging CIS infrastructure is the policy arena. New technologies create new capabilities and new ways of organizing an institution's mission and information resources and services. In some cases these new ways will test and even render obsolete many of higher education's most important institutional policies. Policy impacts will be felt in a number of areas, including access to information, information privacy, information security, and ownership issues.

Access to Information. Federal and state statutes, myriad regulations, and institutional policies highly regulate access to institutional records, rightly so because colleges and universities are variously the custodians of young people who are entering adulthood, of patients requiring tertiary care in their medical centers, of human subjects in research protocols, and so forth. The new CIS infrastructure will make it relatively easy and cost effective to acquire, store, and manage volumes of information about the institution's stakeholders.

New software capabilities, service delivery strategies, and practices will make it possible to deliver personalized and customized services for institutional constituents, based on detailed information about the roles such constituents play. One student may not, for example, have access to certain core institutional data repositories. Another student, for example, a journalist with the daily campus newspaper, may have special access privileges. Finally, a third student, this one the president of the student governing body and a student regent, may have differing authorities based on this unique combination of roles. In environments in which information and services are organized for self-service by empowered members of the institutional community, the rules and logistics of managing the complex role-based authorizations within the institution will be a new area of importance, complexity, and expense.

Information Privacy. Similarly, colleges and universities will need to incorporate safeguards in the CIS infrastructure to ensure the privacy of members of the community. New efforts to organize systems and information to customize and personalize services will raise new concerns about the institution's rights to "repurpose" personal information collected for other purposes. New policies will need to balance individual privacy with new and complex institutional objectives and purposes to simplify, customize, and personalize service offerings. Most students would value expert systems that create model curricula based on their profiled preferences or academic histories. These systems will enhance the academic counseling process. Such systems also depend on tracking student choice and grade performance in new and unexpected ways. For some students such new ways may challenge the trust that students place in our institutions.

Information Security. Information security is closely related to information privacy and will demand the creation of new policies to protect the institution and its constituents. The rise of the Internet and other key elements of the CIS infrastructure has meant that—in a virtual sense—all sorts of new people will visit your institution. University Web sites such as those at the universities of Washington, Wisconsin, and Minnesota are among the most frequently visited sites in the world. Although such popularity can create new and politically potent supporters for the institution, it can also attract those who continually probe the campus network looking for openings to launch denial-of-service attacks, engage in theft of personal information, damage institutional computing and information resources, and perform other criminal activities. Security policies must recognize these threats and protect the institution against them while protecting basic rights of speech and expression consistent with higher education's purposes.

Ownership of Faculty Course Materials. The evolving CIS infrastructure makes it possible for a university or college to deliver its core activity of instruction across time zones and geographies. It is not clear in such an environment whether information content becomes "king," as some argue, or whether content comes to behave more like a commodity. In either scenario profound impacts can be felt concerning the course materials that faculty members have developed to support their instruction. When courses are modified for use across networks, their cost of production and their revenue potential are altered. Under such conditions institutions are expressing new levels of interest in a share of ownership of such materials, and individual faculty often demonstrate a greater proprietary concern about such materials. Institutions must in these environments develop equitable policies and practices to reflect the new realities of courses produced for delivery over networks.

Putting Humpty Dumpty Back Together Again: Higher Education Practices and Frontiers in a Context of Disruption

Much has been written regarding the ways in which disruptive technological changes force changes to businesses and industries. Much of this literature is apocalyptic in tone and likens higher education to health care, an industry that has been revolutionized by regulatory and technological change. Peering through a "very foggy crystal ball," EDUCAUSE president Brian Hawkins (2000, p. 65) asserts these axioms about information technology's impact on higher education:

- New technology affords exciting opportunities for more effective teaching.
- New technology offers a scalability that is greatly needed.
- New technology will transform higher education as we know it today.

On the basis of these axioms and of his assessment of the higher education landscape Hawkins goes on to make some credible forecasts, including the following:

- New markets will be smaller than predicted.
- Residential campuses will continue to be significant.
- An erosion of traditional markets will occur.
- Individual campuses will not effectively participate as stand-alone entities.
- The new marketplace will be associated with new models of faculty motivation.
- Technology will transform college and university operations.

This forecast creates a powerful impression about the future context that colleges and universities operate within.

At the macroeconomic level this context is characterized by increased competition. Winston and Zimmerman (2000) describe the current environment of tuition discounting as tantamount to a positional arms race for the globe's finest students. Private residential institutions, as Hawkins (2000) suggests, depend increasingly on segmented markets for their prosperity or even survival. Technology has also created new opportunities for a variety of competitors to simultaneously incorporate both new tools and pedagogy and eschew the investments in plant and infrastructure that are required by comprehensive, site-based institutions. Yale University's Collis (1999, 2000) suggests that some of these new providers will quietly establish beachheads in relatively "peripheral" niches (continuing education, general education, remedial education, and so on) but will over the long term develop the skill and market acceptance to move up the education food chain. Finally, major new initiatives such as the e-Army initiative, Universitas21, and others bear witness to Hawkins's forecast that the future higher education landscape will be influenced by the emergence of powerful educational consortia.

Within the campus a number of leading institutions herald the emergence of the information or knowledge-based organization (Sveily, 1997) The information-based organization is a metaphor that describes a CIS infrastructure that has been optimized for ergonomic integration, ubiquitous and secure access, personalization, and self-service use by an educated and empowered institutional community. This is a powerful metaphor. Conceptually, the technological framework that supports this vision proposes a Web-based system (portal) that recognizes individual users and tailors accessible information and services to the needs, interests, and authorities of each individual. Such a conceptual framework is compelling and sounds simple. Although its goal is indeed simplification, integrating such a new infrastructure with existing college and university practices is difficult in the extreme.

Changing Expectations. In the context of a changing CIS infrastructure college and university practices are being driven by changing expectations. In today's environment early technology adopters carry cell phones and palm-held computers and expect nothing less than a constant stream of information that has been tailored to meet the demands of their busy lives. In the academic context students want to conduct all institutional "administrivia" over the Internet, phone, desktop, or most convenient device twenty-four hours a day, seven days a week. Most institutions are variously a mile or a millennium from delivering such an environment in practice. Increasingly, students will come to expect (and demand) all course materials on the Web. They will also become adept at identifying useful online course supplements that can help them learn (through simulation, virtual reality, or other technologies) in ways that best reflect their learning styles and pace. Before long students will come to expect a degree of instructional personalization that cannot likely be contained within our current concept of the academic calendar.

Faculty, parents, staff, and alumni are likely to become similarly voracious in their expectations of an institution's CIS infrastructure. They will expect grade reporting, student loan payment and tracking, class registration, and contract administration processes to operate automatically, to be completely integrated and personalized to their users, and to be operated twenty-four hours a day, seven days a week, 365 days a year. These expectations should not come as a surprise because they correspond with current expectations of private enterprise. Today, one can be notified by digital cell phones of flight delays and cancellations, of dining options, and so on. We now download daily newspapers to our wireless handheld computers, so why can't we have our class schedules, grant balances, and campus events calendars that way as well?

Changing Practices and New Frontiers: When Worlds Collide. The changing landscape of the CIS infrastructure will affect college and university practices in several significant arenas.

Leadership, Organization, and Governance. The college and university political system, variously described as *adhocracies, cottage industries,* or *organized anarchies,* will need to explore the development of new institutional compacts that will guide the growth of an integrated CIS infrastructure. Fiefdoms that evolve around the ownership of information, processes, Web sites, and the like will be unlikely to realize the vision of the information-based organization described here. Institutional leaders will need to explore new ways of confederating campus leaders in ways that allow local campus units to continue to operate services and processes, but within agreed-upon frameworks and standards that will create the sense of institutional integrity that campus constituents will demand. One leader at the University of Minnesota has even suggested the need for institutional constitutions that regulate the rights and responsibilities and the members of the campus community in the new information-based organizational context.

Leadership and followership change in organizations designed around empowerment and access to information. Most colleges and universities continue to rely on specialists who understand the complex rules and regulations that guide access to student records, care of laboratory animals, employee benefit entitlements, and the like. As a result of tremendous regulation and fear of lawsuits these campus experts have generally been charged with providing services while protecting the institution against any number of risks. In such environments the mastery of rules and reduction of risk takes precedence over service, and service suffers. In an information-based organization complex rules are rendered either transparently into the information systems of the institution or are explained in a clear and concise manner so that the consumer of a service can invoke that service without invoking an expert. At the University of California, San Diego, teams of journalists are tasked with working with the owners of the institution's key business processes in an effort to render the policy infrastructure transparent and user friendly.

The information-based organization that emerges from the new infra-structure assumes that institutions are aligned around this vision of inte-gration, personalization, and self-service. Such alignment suggests the need for an organizational culture that is team based and multidisciplinary. It also suggests the increasing need for skilled generalists and a concomitant decreasing reliance on specialists. This lack of skilled generalists is another gap in practice that needs to be managed. Finally, the leadership of the information-based organization will demand extraordinary skill in creating the incentives, training opportunities, technology investments, and trust to create a vision, engage key leaders of the institution in the vision, remove barriers, and above else, give people the authority to make the vision hap-pen. The leaders of this new world will lead by example and will work to reshape the policy environment in ways that reinforce both the vision and the behaviors of those on whom the vision depends.

Cooperation and Competition. The point has been made that the shift in the CIS infrastructure is heightening the level of competition in higher education. A smaller number of U.S. institutions garner a growing share of the world's college-bound high school graduates. Similarly, a small number of institutions control most of the endowment resources in higher educa-tion, and their faculty garner most of the private- and public-sponsored research funding. New for-profit entities enter and exit the marketplace with increasing regularity. Microsoft and Cisco set international curricular stan-dards through their software certification programs. Although Hawkins is likely correct that new markets will be smaller than expected in the heyday of dot-com enthusiasm, it is also correct that the new infrastructure will make new modes of teaching and learning possible and will change the eco-nomics of scale in higher education. These changes suggest that competi-tion will only intensify over time and that some institutions that fail to adapt in one way or another to changing conditions will themselves fail.

Ironically, perhaps, the most promising strategy to lend strength to institutions operating in the promising but complex environment described is cooperation. If indeed the changing CIS infrastructure is likely to trans-form higher education's operations and the practices that support them, and if further, this infrastructure will be costly in financial and political terms, will it not be wise to consider new cooperative arrangements? Such new arrangements can spread the risks and shortening life cycles of the infra-structure over a larger financial base. Similarly, such arrangements can spread the risk of procedural innovation (new processes, new pedagogies, and so on) of this larger base. New forms of collaboration make it possible for institutional partners to focus on what really creates institutional dis-tinction and comparative advantage. For too long, colleges and universities have trumpeted one another's idiosyncrasies in order to justify the need for distinctive payroll systems, accounts receivable operations, grant accounting systems, and so forth. Much like contemporary automotive engineering, the new CIS infrastructure will likely be built as software components that are integrated by common standards to a portal-like Web framework. If true, this makes it possible for institutions to source complex technical solutions from the commercial marketplace and from other institutions, again reinforcing the potential presented by new forms of collaboration. Finally, new consortia and other forms of collaboration make possible breaking the bonds of complex rules and practices. This can be valuable to leaders who are attempting to manage change in environments steeped in risk-averse cultures of rules and experts. It is perhaps axiomatic to observe that the barriers to realizing the promise presented by the changing CIS infrastructure are far more likely to be found in the organizational, leadership, and policy arenas than in the technology and resources domains. New forms of collaboration, bound often in contracts and performance agreements can provide powerful counterincentives to the campus-based rewards that often drive behaviors that are antithetical to constructive change.

Summing Up

The changing CIS infrastructure will affect higher education's practices and future in significant ways. Transformational rhetoric is not hyperbolic. Traditional residential institutions are likely to continue to serve the needs of a growing population in need of postsecondary education, although competition will likely intensify. Competitive success will depend in part on a strategy of organizing around an increasingly segmented marketplace. New information technologies will make it possible to deliver the core college and university mission in new and exciting ways. One vision suggests the creation of an information-based college or university. The information-based institution simplifies the policy environment radically, making it possible to imbed most complex rules in the information systems themselves. Once imbedded in this fashion, systems can be organized and integrated in ways that allow those who use institutional services to consume these services directly via the Web. In this vision institutional processes and services are organized around a common vision for security, access, navigation, and Web functionality. Through the incorporation of standards such a vision makes it possible to develop and deploy services in a confederated fashion, much as automobile manufacturers assemble cars using component parts created to conform to a set of industry standards. The information-based organization and the infrastructure supporting it create the potential to liberate the members of the institutional community from the tyranny and oppression of institutional rules, processes, and administrivia.

Such new freedom creates the potential for a renaissance in the institutions' primary roles of teaching, discovery, patient care, and service. Rising expectations combined with new technological capabilities and new competition will foster new forms of cooperation among traditional colleges and universities. These collaborations, too, carry with them both the potential to transform and more important, the potential to enhance higher education's role and performance in an era that will demand greater education attainment and outcomes.

References

Christensen, C. *The Innovator's Dilemma: When New Technologies Cause Great Firms to Fail.* Cambridge, Mass.: Harvard Business School Press, 1997.

Collis, D. "When Industries Change: Scenarios for Higher Education." In M. E. Devlin and J. W. Meyerson (eds.), *Forum Futures, 1999 Papers.* Cambridge, Mass.: Forum, 1999.

Collis, D. "When Industries Change, Revisited: New Scenarios for Higher Education." In M. E. Devlin and J. E. Meyerson (eds.), *Forum Futures, 2000 Papers.* San Francisco: Jossey-Bass, 2001.

Galbreath, J. *Managing Complex Organizations.* New York: Addison-Wesley, 1974.

Gershenfeld, N. *When Things Start to Think.* New York: Henry Holt, 1999.

Hawkins, B. L. "Technology, Education, and a Very Foggy Crystal Ball." *EDUCAUSE Review,* 2000, *35*(6), 65–73.

McLuhan, M. "The Medium Is the Message." In *Understanding Media: The Extensions of Man.* New York: McGraw Hill, 1964.

Rockart, J. *Computers and the Learning Process in Higher Education: A Report Prepared for the Carnegie Commission on Higher Education.* New York: McGraw-Hill, 1975.

Simon, H. A. *Administrative Behavior.* (2nd ed.) New York: Free Press, 1965.

Sveily, K. E. *The New Organizational Wealth.* San Francisco: Berritt-Koehler, 1997.

Trow, M. "Notes on the Development of Information Technology in Higher Education." *Daedelus,* 1997, *126*(4), 293–314.

Winston, G., and Zimmerman, D. "Where Is Aggressive Price Competition Taking Higher Education?" *Change Magazine,* 2000, *32*(4), 10–18.

RICHARD N. KATZ is vice president of EDUCAUSE in Boulder, Colorado.

INDEX

Academic freedom, 72
Academic/instruction function, 18
Academy, nature of, 3
Access, 21–22, 98–99: future of, 38
Access policies, 74. *See also* Computer network policies
Adhocracies, 97, 102
Administrative overhead, 69
American Library Association Intellectual Freedom Committee, "Guidelines for the Development and Implementation of Policies, Regulations and Procedures Affecting Access to Library Materials, Services, and Facilities," 78
Americans with Disabilities Act, 37, 54
Analog technology, 34
Anarchical institution, 88
Antolovic', Laurie G., 61
Application sharing, 12

Bandwidth, 38, 45, 67, 84
Bennis, W., 86
Berquist, W. H., 88–89
Biederman, P., 86
Birnbaum, R., 89, 92
Bridges, 46
Budget, 21, 98: elements of, 65–69; expenses, 66–69; life-cycle funding, 98; plans and, 61–62; revenues, 65–66
Bureaucratic institution, 88
Bush, Vannevar, 91

Campus, 3, 11. *See also* Modern campus
Capital expenses, 66–67
Carnegie Foundation for the Advancement of Teaching, 4
Charge-back service, 65
Chief information officer (CIO), 87
A Choice of Transformations for the Twenty-First-Century University (Duderstadt), 4
Clark, R. H., 83
Coaxial cable, 42
Collaboration model/tools, 7, 14
Collegial culture/institution, 88
Collis, D., 101
Communication and information systems infrastructure: access to, 21–22; assessment of, 24–25; budget, 21; as change driver, 95; change pressures on, 83–84; devices, 21, 95–96; elements of, 20–21; equilibrium, 23; future of, 69; Gilder's new laws for, 84–85; leadership and, 91; maturity of, 22–24; model of, 20–21; networks, 21, 96; policies and, 21; skills, 21, 96–98. *See also* Budget; Leadership
Communication tools, 14
Community service model, 6
Computer network policies, 71–76, 98–99: acceptable and responsible use, 72–74; access policies, 74, 98–99; civility in cyberspace, 79; common sense and netiquette, 73; content, 72; course copyright, 74–76; disabilities, 74; e-commerce policies, 77; ethics, 72; fair use, 72–73; home access, 74; passwords, 74; policy development, 77–78; privacy, 73, 99; security, 74, 99; technology resources, 73; telecommunications policies, 76–77
Computers, 30–31: laptop programs, 31–32
Content, academic freedom and, 72
Contingency leadership, 89
Contract law, 73
Convergence of technology, 63–64
Copyright, 73: academic exception, 75; background of, 75; commonsense approach to, 76; course copyright, 74–76, 100; evolving approaches to, 76; independent contractors, 75; ownership options, 75–76; unbundling option, 76; works-for-hire, 75
Core IT workforce. *See* Information technology (IT) workforce
Cost-accounting standards, 65
Cottage industries, 102
Course copyright, 74–76, 100
Course management system, 13–14
Critical mass, 23, 52
Customer expectations, 62–63
Cyberspace, ten principles of civility in, 79

SINGLE ISSUE SALE

For a limited time save 10% on single issues! Save an additional 10% when you purchase three or more single issues. Each issue is normally 27^{00}.

Please see the next page for a complete listing of available back issues.

Mail or fax this completed form to: Jossey-Bass, A Wiley Company
989 Market Street • Fifth Floor • San Francisco CA 94103-1741

CALL OR FAX

Phone 888-378-2537 or 415-433-1740 *or Fax* 800-605-2665 or 415-433-4611 (*attn customer service*)

BE SURE TO USE PRIORITY CODE ND2 TO GUARANTEE YOUR DISCOUNT!

Please send me the following issues at 24^{30} each.

Important: please include series initials and issue number, such as HE114

1. HE _____

_____

_____

$ _____ TOTAL for single issues ($24^{30} each)

_____ LESS 10% if ordering 3 or more issues

_____ SHIPPING CHARGES: SURFACE   Domestic   Canadian

                         First Item $5.00 $6.50

                Each Add'l Item $3.00 $3.00

      For next-day and second-day delivery rates, call the number listed above.

$ _____ TOTAL (Add appropriate sales tax for your state. Canadian residents add GST)

❏ Payment enclosed (U.S. check or money order only)

❏ VISA, MC, AmEx Discover Card # _____ Exp. date _____

Signature _____

Day phone _____

❏ Bill me (U.S. institutional orders only. Purchase order required)

Purchase order # _____

      Federal Tax ID. 135593032   GST 89102 8052

Name _____

Address _____

_____

Phone _____ E-mail _____

For more information about Jossey-Bass, visit our website at: www.josseybass.com

OFFER EXPIRES FEBRUARY 28, 2002.   **PRIORITY CODE = ND2**

community within individual courses to the creative use physical space, information technology, living-learning communities, and experiential education programs.
ISBN: 0-7879-5340-7

HE108   **Promising Practices in Recruitment, Remediation, and Retention**
Gerald H. Gaither
Identifies the best practices for recruitment, remediation, and retention, describing lessons learned from innovative and successful programs across the nation, and shows how to adapt these efforts to today's diverse populations and technological possibilities.
ISBN: 0-7879-4860-8

HE107   **Roles and Responsibilities of the Chief Financial Officer**
Lucie Lapovsky, Mary P. McKeoan-Moak
Offers strategies for balancing the operating and capital budgets, maximizing net enrollment revenues, containing costs, planning for the resource needs of technology, identifying and managing risks, and investing the endowment wisely.
ISBN: 0-7879-4859-4

HE106   **Best Practices in Higher Education Consortia: How Institutions Can Work Together**
Lawrence G. Dotolo, Jean T. Strandness
Gives detailed accounts of activities and programs that existing consortia have already refined, providing practical models that can be replicated or modified by other institutions, and describes how to start and sustain a consortium.
ISBN: 0-7879-4858-6

HE105   **Reconceptualizing the Collegiate Ideal**
J. Douglas Toma, Adrianna J. Kezar
Explores how administration, student affairs, and faculty work can work together to redefine the collegiate ideal, incorporating the developmental needs of a diverse student body and the changes in higher education's delivery and purpose.
ISBN: 0-7879-4857-8

HE104   **The Growing Use of Part-Time Faculty: Understanding the Causes and Effects**
David W. Leslie
Presents analyses of the changes in academic work, in faculty careers, and in the economic conditions in higher education that are associated with the shift away from full-time academic jobs. Issues for research, policy, and practices are also discussed.
ISBN: 0-7879-4249-9

HE103   **Enhancing Productivity: Administrative, Instructional and Technological Strategies**
James E. Groccia, Judith E. Miller
Presents a multi-faceted approach for enhancing productivity that emphasizes both cost-effectiveness and the importance of bringing together all segments of the educational economy—institutions, faculty, students, and society—to achieve long-term productivity gains.
ISBN: 0-7879-4248-0

HE102 **Minority-Serving Institutions: Distinct Purposes, Common Goals**
Jamie P. Merisotis, Colleen T. O'Brien
Serves as a primer on the growing group of minority-serving institutions, with the goal of educating leaders at mainstream institutions, analysts, and those at minority-serving institutions themselves about their distinct purposes and common goals.
ISBN: 0-7879-4246-4

HE101 **The Experience of Being in Graduate School: An Exploration**
Melissa S. Anderson
Addresses the graduate experience from the standpoint of the students themselves. Presents what students have reported about their experience through interviews, surveys, ongoing discussions, and autobiographies.
ISBN: 0-7879-4247-2

HE100 **The Campus-Level Impact of Assessment: Progress, Problems, and Possibilities**
Peter J. Gray, Trudy W. Banta
Explores successful assessment efforts, and answers questions about why some efforts succeed and others don't. Provides proven practices and lessons learned in the development of effective assessment programs.
ISBN: 0-7879-9824-9

HE99 **Rethinking the Dissertation Process: Tackling Personal and Institutional Obstacles**
Lester F. Goodchild, Kathy E. Green, Elinor L. Katz, Raymond C. Kluever
Identifies the institutional patterns and support structures that enhance the dissertation process, and describes how the introduction of dissertation-stage financial support and workshops can quicken completion rates.
ISBN: 0-7879-9889-3

HE98 **The Professional School Dean: Meeting the Leadership Challenges**
Michael J. Austin, Frederick L. Ahearn, Richard A. English
Focuses on the demanding leadership roles assumed by deans of social work, law, engineering, nursing, and divinity, providing case illustrations that illuminate the deanship experience at other professional schools.
ISBN: 0-7879-9849-4

HE97 **The University's Role in Economic Development: From Research to Outreach**
James P. Pappas
Offers models the academy can use to foster the ability to harness the research and educational resources of higher education institutions as well as the potential of state and land-grant universities to provide direct services for local and regional economic development through outreach missions.
ISBN: 0-7879-9890-7

HE96 **Preparing Competent College Graduates: Setting New and Higher Expectations for Student Learning**
Elizabeth A. Jones
Using the results of a nationwide study, this volume identifies specific ways institutions can help undergraduates attain the advanced thinking, communication, and problem-solving skills needed in today's society and workplace.
ISBN: 0-7879-9823-0